THEATRE KIDS

THEATRE KIDS

A TRUE TALE OF
OFF-OFF-BROADWAY

JOHN DEVORE

APPLAUSE
THEATRE & CINEMA BOOKS
Essex, Connecticut

APPLAUSE
THEATRE & CINEMA BOOKS

An imprint of Globe Pequot, the trade division of
The Rowman & Littlefield Publishing Group, Inc.
4501 Forbes Blvd., Ste. 200
Lanham, MD 20706
www.rowman.com

Distributed by NATIONAL BOOK NETWORK

British Library Cataloguing in Publication Information available

Library of Congress Cataloging-in-Publication Data

Names: DeVore, John (Editor), author.
Title: Theatre kids : a true tale of off-off Broadway / John DeVore.
Description: Essex, Connecticut : Applause Press, 2024.
Identifiers: LCCN 2024008087 (print) | LCCN 2024008088 (ebook) | ISBN
 9781493077762 (cloth) | ISBN 9781493077779 (epub)
Subjects: LCSH: DeVore, John (Editor). | Actors—New York (State)—New
 York—Biography. | Theater—New York (State)—New York—Biography. |
 LCGFT: Autobiographies. | Humor.
Classification: LCC PN2287.D458 A3 2024 (print) | LCC PN2287.D458 (ebook)
 | DDC 792.02/8092 [B]—dc23/eng/20240307
LC record available at https://lccn.loc.gov/2024008087
LC ebook record available at https://lccn.loc.gov/2024008088

♾️™ The paper used in this publication meets the minimum requirements of American
National Standard for Information Sciences—Permanence of Paper for Printed Library
Materials, ANSI/NISO Z39.48-1992

To Mr. Boyd

"We're born alone, we live alone, we die alone. Only through our love and friendship can we create the illusion for the moment that we're not alone."

—ORSON WELLES, THEATRE KID

I
MY LIFE IN ART

Lights up on a small theater in Brooklyn, New York. Enter John DeVore, late forties. His hair and beard are streaked with gray. He stands in a spotlight center stage and says:

My name is John, and I'm a theatre kid. I'm a theatre kid the way a raccoon is a raccoon, or a pineapple is a pineapple. I like to think of it as my astrological sign, something about me that is fixed. It is who I am and I had little choice in the matter.

During one of my very first school plays, a teacher suggested I had been bitten by the acting bug, contracting a virus with no known cure. But I knew better: I had been screaming for attention since I was born. If I could have been the opposite of a theatre kid, I would have. But I can't be who I'm not. I'm pretty sure the opposite of a theatre kid is a Dallas Cowboys fan.

Being a theatre kid is like that Groucho joke about not wanting to join a club that would have you as a member. That's my experience, at least. I've never been a joiner. If I could change that about me, I would. I want to be loved and left alone at the same time. That is my default setting. My therapist is always telling me to open my heart to other people, and my usual response to his gentle requests is, "I'm trying, Gary."

I once denied being a theatre kid, like how the apostle Peter repeatedly lied when asked by the mob if he knew Jesus. My denial happened years ago, in the late aughts. 2008? Right before the economy cratered. Those were dark times for me. I had gone on an impromptu weeknight bender with a former colleague—a lonely old journalist with a talent for sniffing out bullshit and a sickening thirst for crème de menthe—who suspected I had acted in high school or college. I just laughed him off. Me? A theatre kid? No.

And my ruse would have worked had we not stumbled, piss-drunk, into a nearly empty karaoke bar and had I not insisted on performing a sloppy, surprisingly poignant rendition of the popular torch song "On My Own" from the blockbuster 1987 Broadway mega-musical *Les Misérables,* which, if you're not aware, is a weepy, blood-and-thunder pop opera written by Claude-Michel Schönberg and Alain Boubli and based on Victor Hugo's nineteenth-century novel about poor French vagrants suffering beautifully.

"On My Own" is sung by forlorn street waif Eponine, who pines after handsome revolutionary Marius. Marius's heart belongs to Cosette, the adopted daughter of our hero, ex-convict Jean Valjean. Eponine is a lonely victim of unrequited love, and later, she dies in Marius's arms, fulfilling the deepest, darkest, most pathetic fantasy of anyone who has ever longed for someone they could never have.

My former colleague could see the truth in my tear-filled eyes as I sang with everything I had. I couldn't help myself. I was feeling it. I sang like I was competing for a Tony Award. I did that thing Broadway divas do where they slowly push one jazz hand toward the heavens as the emotions swell. I was in church, and from the back pew, I could hear him laughing and pointing at me, like I was a fool. He knew a theatre kid when he saw one.

Like I said: dark times.

And how can you tell if someone you know, or even love, is a theatre kid? Ask yourself this: Do they take a lot of selfies? Do. They. Enunciate. Every. Word? Do they frequently sigh heavily? Do they talk about themselves and their manifold feelings incessantly? These are just a few of the signs. Do they spell it t-h-e-a-t-r-e instead of t-h-e-a-t-e-r? That's a good one. Only a true theatre kid spells it "theatre." A "theater" is where you watch "theatre." You see? No? This difference matters, and if you don't think it does, you're probably not a theatre kid, which may come as a relief to many of you.

Now I need you to know that I know that t-h-e-a-t-r-e is just the British spelling of the word. But I much prefer the other explanation, don't you? It's more romantic. The theatre is an ancient art, a sacred, almost holy, occupation.

It's a way to teach moral lessons and to celebrate the human condition; it's a story full of sound and fury that can levitate you or knock you sideways. The theatre is a spirit, and the theater is where you sit and cough politely, and then the curtain rises. There might not even be a curtain. A theater can be a space, any space. A storefront, an apartment living room, a parking lot.

This wisdom has been passed down from theatre kid to theatre kid from time immemorial. It was a veteran of my high school's drama program who taught me the difference between theatre and theater. She was a full year older than me, but she knew things. I thought she was brilliant. I remember listening to her intently: theatre was life. This lesson probably happened over cups of creamy, sugary coffee and plates of baklava at the local twenty-four-hour diner where all the theatre kids at my high school would go to celebrate after a successful production—a one-act or the spring musical.

We'd pour into the diner like an army of frogs, laughing and talking a mile a minute and singing show tunes and the poor servers endured our overbearing youthful cheerfulness. My true theatre education happened either at that diner or backstage, during rehearsal breaks, and these impromptu lectures are the closest thing to an oral tradition in action I've ever encountered.

These sixteen-year-old elders patiently explained the superstitions and rules of the theatre, and I did the same when it was my turn to pass on the lore. I remember the rules like commandments: never whistle backstage or say the name of Shakespeare's famous tragedy about that Scottish couple who make a series of poorly thought-out career decisions. Both of those things are bad luck.

Saying "good luck" is also bad luck. You're supposed to say "break a leg." There are all sorts of explanations as to what that phrase means. I was told, over a plate of french fries, that in ye olden times, the mechanism that raised and lowered the curtains was called a "leg," and so to break that device would mean that the audience cheered for so many encores, the curtain went up and down and up and down until it broke. Is that true? I have no idea. That's just how I heard it.

Here are a few more sacred rules: Give flowers after a performance, not before. Always open the stage door for one of your fellow castmates and invite them to enter first with a graceful bow. One of my favorites warns against putting your shoes on any table backstage. Don't do that. Why? I don't think you want to find out.

There were also practical, straightforward rules about rehearsal and being part of a production. Always be on time. ("If you're ten minutes early, you're on time. If you're on time, you're late." That was the mantra. I was told to repeat it and to repeat it.) Don't skip rehearsal. Memorize your lines. Stretch before every performance, and drink nothing but hot water with lemon juice and honey if you catch a cold. And never, ever become romantically involved with someone in the cast, a rule that was broken during every production at my high school, sometimes multiple times. Show romances were a huge no-no. This rule was meant to keep rehearsals drama-free, but rehearsals are intense and intimate, and it's almost impossible to keep theatre kids from trying to make out with other theatre kids.

Show romances—also known as "showmances"—were looked down on, even by those who had show romances, and the only exceptions were hook-ups between cast and crew, which worked in my favor. I will always be a sucker for a girl who can use power tools because I cannot use power tools, and I fell for stage managers and set builders. A boy never hit on me, but I was ready for it, just in case, and had practiced a flattered "I like you, but I don't like-like you" speech in the mirror. I never got to perform that speech, which disappointed me. A few years later, in college, a beautiful man kissed me on the dance floor of a party. It was a deep and playful kiss, and before I could stammer "I like you, but I don't . . ." he had disappeared into the crowd, and now that I think about it, that was disappointing too.

When I was a senior I gave the newbies at the diner a variation of the speech I was given in ninth grade. It went something like: "Look around at this table. These are the friends you'll have for the rest of your life." That wasn't true, but in the moment, it felt true, and that's good enough. I also passed along to them what was passed to me, from senior to frosh, and that's always, always attend the closing-night cast party, and stay until the very end.

* * *

The sobriquet "theatre kid" wasn't used in the late '80s, when I was a mutating adolescent. That wasn't the term used to describe the queens, goobers, goth freaks, and human tornadoes who populated drama clubs, the social lint trap of high schools everywhere. "Theatre kid" didn't become a thing until years later, and we were all retroactively re-anointed.

No. We were called "drama queers," and I was happy to be called a "drama queer," even though the blatant homophobia went over my head. It didn't occur to me at the time that "queer" was derogatory, a slur. I thought they meant it in the *Alice in Wonderland* sense. You know: curious, odd, special. I was all of those things. I was strange and extraordinary, like Sally Bowles. She's the main character in the musical *Cabaret*.

We were also occasionally referred to as thespians, which is a very funny word to some teenagers, usually the same ones who laugh at the name of the planet Uranus. During my senior year, I became a member of The International Thespian Society, the only honor society I would qualify for, and I suddenly found the word thespian to be terribly dignified.

But I was proud to be a drama queer—a theatre kid. Even though we were the butt of countless jokes told by civilians. Not much has changed, either. I know those two words are used as an insult on social media. To be a theatre kid is to be obnoxious. You're a not-so-complicated mix of "please love me" and "I hate myself." But if you are an overly emotional or anxious teen, you can easily find your people—look for the loud ones.

One of my best friends in drama club came out of the closet during our junior year, which took great courage for him at that miserable moment in history, when grown adults told other adults that gay people spread diseases like rats. But he didn't tell me for months.

There was another word for "drama queer," a more openly hateful one favored by the popular boys. It's an "F" word and not the fun one. I was thankful to have the small group of friends that I did, but I was still a confused, lonely, thoughtless straight boy, and there were times I used the word "faggot," casually, or to show off, and it wasn't until I learned that friend of mine, who I loved so much, hesitated to tell me who he really was did I realize that people listen to you, even when you don't think they do. People listen, so be careful what you say because you are responsible for what you say, whether you mean what you say or not. When he eventually told me his secret, I was relieved. I thought he was going to tell me that he didn't want to be my friend anymore.

I won't argue that theatre kids can't be annoying, desperate for attention, self-centered, and overemotional. They try too hard. But all my favorite people are theatre kids. They are earnest to a fault, loyal, accepting, horny as hell, petty, bitter, and prone to monologues. Theatre kids are show-offs. We bleed easily. We love vodka and cigarettes and poorly rolled joints. We fall in love intensely and rage when betrayed. Life can be pretty emotional, and it helps to know people who understand that deeply.

And then there are the musicals. I know Broadway show tunes make most people roll their eyes, but musicals were the electrical current that lit the hearts of all my noisy, motormouthed, tempestuous friends. Our national anthem was "One Day More," the rousing, fist-pumping anthem sung by student revolutionaries and their allies on the eve of a mass uprising that ends

Act I of *Les Misérables* on a defiant note of faith in what tomorrow can bring. (I hate to spoil the musical, but it brings death and failure.)

My mom loved musicals too. All the usual suspects: *Fiddler on the Roof. Little Shop of Horrors.* (She couldn't get enough of "Suddenly Seymour" from that show, a stirring duet between flower shop lonelyheart Audrey and Seymour, the hapless dweeb who nurtures a man-eating plant from another planet. "Suddenly Seymour" is a lovely song about the transformative power of love.) She had a special place in her heart for *Jesus Christ Superstar*, Andrew Lloyd Webber's true masterpiece. I was a fan of his *The Phantom of the Opera*, which was the closest thing musical theatre has to Batman. But *Jesus Christ Superstar* appealed to the rebel Catholic inside my mom, a faithful church member who believed women should be priests. The most radical part of the show was the idea that Judas wasn't such a bad guy, and maybe he deserved forgiveness.

Anyway, *Jesus Christ Superstar* rocked. I'm not always the most confident performer, but I can sing the gritty power ballad "Gethsemane" at a moment's notice.

The drama queers were obnoxious but easy to avoid, and the whole school did, for the most part. We could be found sitting on the cold linoleum floors outside the theater, gossiping, giggling, and giving each other back massages. Platonic group snuggles were a cherished activity only occasionally broken up by adults. If you wanted a cigarette, you could bum one from the DQs out in the parking lot; I was not part of the smokers' club yet.

Luckily for civilians, you could tell a drama queer by how they dressed; you could see us coming. We wore mascara. Combat boots. Second-hand suit vests and long scarves. I remember one guy who dressed like a medieval poet. Fedoras were in, and so were trench coats. The girls loved flowery skirts, and so did some of the boys. My look was standard nerd: oversized T-shirts and baggy pants. Then there were the backstage crew members who all wore the same uniform: black. Just . . . black everything. They were living shadows ready to do the thankless work of making a play happen on time, no applause necessary.

The most prized fashion accessories of all were the walkie-talkies that stage managers were allowed to wield during tech week, five days of chaos and tears that climaxed with opening night. Worn on the hip or carried around like a fashionable handbag, the walkie-talkie blended form and function as orders were shouted from the booth to the backstage.

The school's backstage was a clubhouse for drama queers. I'd spend hours there painting sets, rehearsing, or hanging out. It's also the first place I'd go farther than a kiss—not that far, though, as I didn't lose my virginity until my first year of college when I clumsily climbed on top of my first girlfriend and breathlessly asked, "What do I do next?" and she patiently told me. "First, unwrap a condom."

But the backstage moment I think about the most to this day is peeking from behind the curtains and watching the audience walk to their seats. I was invisible, and a part of me wanted to disappear, to vanish when things got too intense or intimate. I would eventually find other ways to obliterate myself, but peering at friends and family from a distance, in the dark, sufficed at the time.

I didn't always know I was a drama queer at first. I tried out for various clubs during the first few months of high school, but I wasn't into yearbooks or public speaking or science. I tried to be interested in model rockets, but I wasn't. I dutifully signed up to try out for the football team my freshman year, but I was gently steered away from sports by one of the coaches and toward the performing arts, where I found a surprise morsel of courage deep inside me the moment before my very first audition, for a student-directed one-act.

It was a group audition, and the director, an upperclassman who wore jeans and large sweaters and had a mess of midnight-black hair and whom

I would eventually fall madly in love with, asked us to each exit the multi-purpose room where we were all nervously collected, then reenter and try to get the group's attention. I watched the other auditioners complete the assignment: they walked out, and walked back in and introduced themselves. One girl sang a few verses of "Memory" from *Cats*, without a lick of irony.

When it was my turn, I considered running. But I walked out, took a moment, then suddenly pushed the door back open and shouted "UFO!" and pointed, as if killer aliens were sneaking up behind the director. I continued the bit as the room filled with sweet, refreshing laughter. "Look out! Oh my God! Ahhh!"

I don't remember what came over me. It wasn't an instantaneous transformation. The divine light of the theatre didn't blind and change me. No. I was Humpty Dumpty on the wall, not Saul on the road to Damascus. I got a light push.

I had cracked myself open instead, like a geode, and at that moment, I discovered that I was full of glittering crystals inside, purple and pink and blue, and I understood that I was meant to do this thing, theatre, whatever it is. I was a drama queer, and I had been the whole time. After the audition, I was surrounded by new friends. One of them, a girl who wore huge hoop earrings and clogs, hugged me out of nowhere, the first time I had ever let someone who wasn't a family member hug me. It was comforting and arousing and terrifying. I wanted the hug to last forever and to have never happened in the first place.

These were my people. I remember thinking that and didn't even know I had people. Instantly, I was part of a finger-snapping gang who understood me, or pretended to, which is enough sometimes. It was a whirlwind.

I got the part, and it was a small part. It wasn't my first part in a play, but it was my high school debut. I played a cop in the thriller *Sorry Wrong Number*, and I stole the show by answering the phone with a mouth full of powdered donut. The polite opening-night laughter and applause crashed over me like warm waves at the beach.

I followed that performance up as one of three G-men in the classic Kaufman and Hart "wacky family meets a stuck-up family" comedy *You Can't Take It with You*. I wore my fedora cocked to one side.

Then, in another student-directed one-act, I got my biggest part to date: Dr. Sugar in Tennessee Williams's lurid play about madness, lust, and dark family secrets, *Suddenly Last Summer*. In the play, my character is hired to lobotomize one of Williams's fragile damsels, Catherine, a young woman who won't stop "babbling" about the murder of her cousin, a possible sexual predator torn to pieces and eaten by local boys he may or may not have victimized. I remember not understanding the play at all, and there were scenes where I read from the script on stage as if Dr. Sugar was reading a book while, at the same time, talking to Catherine about her trauma. It also had the first and last stage kiss of my career, and I soaked the pits of my oversized dress shirt in the moments leading up to my dry, puckered mouth briefly touching my co-star's trembling lips. It was my first kiss, technically. We were too-stiff children wearing adult clothes, pretending to be traumatized alcoholics, and not understanding one lick of Williams's hothouse dialogue.

A few months later, I would have my first real-life kiss backstage while cuddling with the upperclassman whom I auditioned for as a freshman. We were just friends, but we kissed anyway, and a few weeks later, I found a note in my locker telling me that she was in love with one of the Peters boys and I was on my own.

* * *

McLean High School was mad for football, which suited my dad. He would drag me to Friday night games, hoping that the lights and the cheering and the young gladiators crashing into one another would interest me. It never did. I liked the marching band, especially the costumes. The football team was called The Highlanders and the band included a few stout teens playing the bagpipes and wearing Scottish kilts. That was always fun but everytime we'd go to a game, I'd disappear by the end of the first quarter and spend the rest of the evening eating hot dogs under the bleachers.

But football wasn't my high school's sole social focus—not every parent was obsessed with sports. These were the Virginia suburbs of Washington, D.C. in the '80s, which was an awkward mix of rednecks, hungry political operatives, and educated do-gooders making a modest living trying to change the world inside the dark bowels of the U.S. government. A few wanted their children to study something other than ritualized brain damage.

For years, our school had hired a local theatre director to put on a big musical, and his work was wildly popular. He was affable and had infinite patience. His *Godspell* brought the house down, and made him a legend. When I was a sophomore, though, some ambitious school administrator reached out to a nearby college and hired a grad student to direct something more serious, Sophocles's tragedy *Antigone*, a classic about emotion and reason and defiance and dead bodies. This seemed like a sophisticated choice, and the community came out in full force the first night to behold art.

I was about to encounter experimental multimedia theatre for the first time. The lights went down, and the Talking Heads' folk-punk anxiety ballad "Life During Wartime" was cranked up. Loud. Too loud. For the duration of the song, photographs of war crimes were projected on a movie screen for a stunned audience of moms, dads, and children: emaciated corpses, radiation-burned faces, naked girls running in fear from soldiers, followed by nearly three hours of young actors on stage delivering their lines without emotion on a set inspired by German Expressionism. I was simultaneously bored and awestruck. I could feel the displeasure radiate directly from the crumbled brows of dozens of parents fidgeting in their uncomfortable theater seats.

The production was scandalous, but it ran for the weekend, and then it was never spoken of again. I do not know what happened to the director, but for a few days, at least, he was Prometheus bringing the avant-garde to the suburbs.

Enter Mr. Boyd. The administration decided that a faculty member needed to watch over the drama queers, something a part-time director could not do. Mr. Boyd was qualified. He was an elegant, talented man who sometimes laid across his desk during drama class like a nightclub crooner stretching out on top of a piano and telling us stories of dancing and acting in New York City. As I was told, later, he had moved back to the D.C. area a few years before with his partner, who was dying of AIDS. Mr. Boyd would succumb to the disease at thirty-three, shortly before I graduated. They said he died of pneumonia, but we all knew the truth.

I don't remember exactly when I first met the man. It was early in my senior year. One day, he was just in charge of the drama department. No ceremony. I took his theatre class and he quickly became my favorite teacher. He was black and gay and younger than most of his colleagues, who were not like him. The man measured his words. He knew when to keep his head down and when to shine. He dutifully taught drama and social studies. His most visible contribution to my high school was as director of the school color guard, and he also worked with the marching band. But he was ours. I adored him almost immediately.

I once cheekily called him by his first name, William, a level of familiarity one of my shaggy, laid-back English teachers allowed, and he briskly reminded me that his name was "Mr. Boyd." He was one of the first adult to look me in the eyes and talk to me like I deserved respect. I didn't, but it was nice.

Mr. Boyd was sick the entire time I knew him, but I would never have guessed it. That was his story to tell, and we were just children. What did we know? He was always on time and sharp, and every so often he'd tap-dance for us. He wasn't a show-off but he had skills, and they were delightful. He had spent most of his career acting and dancing professionally up and down the East Coast.

Mr. Boyd never condescended to me. He was blunt, honest, and sarcastic. The kind of sarcasm that disinfects. He was also professional. A trained, seasoned actor and dancer but, also, an educator.

He kept his mustache and haircut tight and clean. Mr. Boyd was not silly but could be if he had to be. And he was generous. Patient. Once, he told me a one-act I had written was almost good, with an eye-roll, and I swooned. I also rewrote it because I had decided he wasn't full of it, like every other grown-up. He would guide me toward rule-breaking playwrights like Christopher Durang and María Irene Fornés. He once made fun of *The Phantom of the Opera*, which surprised me. I didn't know you could mock popular things and do it coolly and savagely. He was, of course, correct that the entire musical is about a stalker.

And he was sly. Usually, the drama department's non-musical production was a stuffy classic or a mild comedy by a playwright like Neil Simon. Mr. Boyd's choice for his inaugural effort as head of the drama department was to stage a contemporary play called *Voices from the High School* by Peter Dee, a collection of two-person scenes and monologues explicitly written for and about teenagers that covered such hot-button topics as alcoholism, teen pregnancy, and abusive fathers.

The play did raise some eyebrows, but the content wasn't any more controversial than Afterschool Specials, which were popular half-hour-long educational TV programs that were usually topical social dramas. Mr. Boyd had also assembled a diverse cast of student actors from different religious backgrounds and ethnicities, which included more than one Mormon and a sarcastic and brilliant troublemaker from the Philippines named Carla. He knew drama queers were cliquey, and he wanted to expose other types of kids to theatre.

There was one scene in the play between two friends nervously talking about something that had just happened between them and whether or not they should do that again. I was cast in one of the roles along with one of my best friends, Fred. Once, Fred and I stood in line for hours outside Tower Records to buy the new Guns N' Roses album at midnight, and we listened to it together in his parents' van for hours and hours, singing every grimy little rock song at the top of our lungs.

Mr. Boyd asked Fred and me if we were okay doing this scene, and we both said yes. He asked if we understood what the scene was about, and Fred and I knew: these characters were in love with each other. We trusted Mr. Boyd, who gave us no direction except to let whatever happened happen.

The first time we performed the scene for an audience, at the end, when Fred's character shyly suggested we again do what we had already done, I was supposed to stare off in the distance, and there would be a blackout. But what I did was steamier: I slowly took off my glasses before looking at him longingly, and when the lights came down, the audience *ooh*ed and *ahh*ed. Mr. Boyd congratulated us both after our first bows. He then took me aside and told me to do that with my glasses again. It was my signature move.

The last time I saw Mr. Boyd, he was emaciated and ashen but defiant. He had been on sick leave but he wanted to work. I greeted him like a demented newsie: "How ya doin', Mr. Boyd?!" He rolled his eyes. We were rehearsing the spring musical of my senior year, the Marx Brothers' very silly, very clever *Animal Crackers*. A popular, and non-controversial, choice. It would be cancelled the moment the news spread that he was gone.

Mr. Boyd had cast me as fast-talking Groucho. Fred was Chico. Another friend of mine, Allan, was Harpo. We sat around a piano in the choir's rehearsal room and practiced Groucho's song "Hello, I Must Be Going" together.

Hello, I must be going
I cannot stay, I came to say, "I must be going."

* * *

Closing-night cast parties are a subspecies of wake, a melancholy fare-well, and a rager, with snacks, all rolled into one. I don't know what my high school's football players, cheerleaders, and fans did after winning a game, which wasn't a frequent occurrence. I was never invited to football parties because I was not a jock, but I like to imagine there was plenty of high-fiving and beer and prom kings and queens hooking up, real all-American stuff.

But the party after a high school play closes? That's sing-a-longs to "I'm Too Sexy" by Right Said Fred and "I Had the Time of My Life" from the sweetly raunchy 1987 movie *Dirty Dancing*. A closing night party is a dozen or more hormonal adolescents exploding like Roman candles, filling a sub-urban living room or basement with light and heat and emotions, so many emotions: gratitude and joy and sadness that it's all over. At closing night par-ties, stage managers bury the hatchet with leading ladies and plans are made for the future, plans that include stardom and revolution. There are happy tears and quiet goodbyes, best friends spooning in hammocks, and couples going for walks around the neighborhood and behind bushes.

If there was booze, it was usually a random bottle of something licorice-flavored snuck in by actors. Or a crew member would spark a joint in the gloom of the backyard. I refused both, every time, in high school, because I feared my mom, who would smell my hair and breath before I could ever make it to my bedroom, no matter what time I got home.

These were still the "Just Say No" years when teen drug use was a national epidemic, or at least, that's what parents and politicians believed. The "turn on, tune in, drop out" '60s were long dead, and in their place was a mor-ally dishonest, two-faced culture that demonized marijuana while celebrating country club drugs like cocaine and martinis. Even I was swept up in the hysteria. I once warned a friend of mine who was getting high regularly that he might overdose and die. My mom was determined to get me through high school without becoming a statistic. And just in case I didn't say "No," she'd be there to sniff me.

There were other teen hellraisers in early 1990s Northern Virginia having sex and drinking liquor, but the drama queers were more into dry humping and Jolt, the heavily caffeinated soda that could melt tooth enamel. We did not throw out-of-control bacchanals. Our parties were wholesome friendship frenzies where nerds could be as weird as they wanted to be. They were usually held at the house of the kid from the wealthiest family, which meant there was probably a pool or a hot tub and the parties usually ended with teens jumping in while nervous parents looked on from afar, or some of us piling into cars and sharing pancakes at the diner. Or they ended the way traditional children's parties end, which is with cake. Then home, before curfew.

The *Voices from the High School* closing-night party was all these things. We all swore to each other we'd remain friends forever, to never lose touch, and we tried.

* * *

When we weren't rehearsing, or breaking into rival high schools to tape up our show posters, or actually putting on a show, my fellow drama queers and I were going to see screenings of *The Rocky Horror Picture Show*.

This was, more or less, a weekly event that combined Catholic Mass with prom—the closest thing to prom I ever got to go to, anyway. It was a blessed drama-queer ritual where a bunch of us would throw boas around our necks and go out on the town, with parental approval.

The 1975 cult classic about a pair of squares who stumble on an orgy in a castle, starring Tim Curry as an intergalactic, gender-bending hedonist who builds the perfect muscle-bound boy toy, was a popular midnight movie—costumed crowds had been showing up during the witching hour constantly since the '70s to shout at the screen.

The movie mixed the sexual revolution with 1950s sci-fi and art-rock like The Velvet Underground. Curry's Dr. Frank-N-Furter, a corsetted disco dandy, wasn't, as his introductory song said, "much of a man by the light of day," but at night he was "one hell of a lover." I was immediately besotted with him. He was captivating. I used to wonder what civilians even did Friday nights if they weren't at *Rocky Horror*.

The first time I went to the movie, per the audience participation liturgy, all "virgins"—anyone who hadn't seen it—were required to stand up in front of the theater and receive a mass mock humping from all the veteran sluts who had seen the movie multiple times, a priesthood made up exclusively of rowdy theatre-loving teenagers from other schools. I shrieked when I was dragged to the front and "devirginized." I was terrified, but I loved it: the outrageous outfits, the makeup, the bumping and grinding.

Every Friday night, sometimes after rehearsal, we'd cram into Fred's van, and while he drove us to the movie, Becky would help me apply candy-red lipstick. She was a true suburban freak, a loyal friend who dressed like Satan's little princess.

I came back again and again for the glam rock and the pansexual vamping. In the theater's darkness, as the screen filled with blood-red fabulousness, I copped feels and was felt up myself. Strange hands in strange places, gentle, exploring, nervous. I don't think my mom ever knew I was stealing her lipstick. (Or maybe she did, but she's never mentioned it.) During those secret hours, I could paint my mouth and feel beautiful. Not handsome. Gorgeous. I could act smooth, not hairy. I could pretend I had long legs. It was a harmless game—a wish. To not be you, just for a little bit. To be surrounded by loved ones and never judged.

* * *

I'll set the scene: I'm talking about my future with my father at the tiny kitchen table of my family's modest ranch-style house, a month before the end of the first Gulf War: February 28, 1991. My mother is standing in the kitchen pretending not to listen while cooking dinner, which would have been huevos rancheros, or enchiladas, or taquitos with corned beef, the kinds of meals she grew up eating in El Paso, Texas—simple, tasty, cheap, extremely Mexican-American. Next to the cutting board, an ashtray full of half-smoked Virginia Slim menthols.

When I tell my dad I want to go to college and study theatre, he sighs. He asks a series of reasonable questions, and I have answers:

"What do you want to do?"

"I want to be a playwright."

"What's your fallback career?"

"Actor." Or vice versa. If one doesn't work out, I can do the other. Easy.

He spent his days in a suit and tie and his nights sitting at that kitchen table in his underwear, smoking cigars and listening to my mom talk about her day and chuckling as she sauteed onions, garlic, and chili powder. But this night, he was listening to me. I had a plan.

I even said that out loud: I have a plan. Don't worry.

My dad sucked on his stogie and brought up my older brother, a proud, tough-as-hell Marine. The Corps had shaped him up and turned him from a directionless teen into a brave member of America's armed forces. But my dad's fundamental pitch was far more practical. If I signed up and joined the Reserve Officers Training Corps, or ROTC, I'd enter the service as a Second Lieutenant and could retire when I was forty, which seemed impossibly old at the time. I'd be dead by then, surely. I told him I'd make a terrible Marine unless the Corps had a drama department.

My old man loved football, politics, and video games, and at best, I only showed interest in one: politics, which is just weaponized theatre. He worked for a U.S. Senator—a wealthy Texan Democrat, the son of oil royalty—so politics was the family business at the time. He considered Dallas Cowboys coach Tom Landry to be a great Texan and American, and Pac-Man was almost a sibling.

U.S. coalition forces' campaign against Iraq had made every father with a teen son stop and think the unthinkable, but thankfully, that war was brief. The sins of the Vietnam War were exorcised that year: America was a winner again. The '90s were a Golden Age for some, but only in retrospect. From 1991 until 2001, the good ol' U.S. of A. was a colossus with a beer belly. Rich, powerful, profoundly stupid. But optimistic.

I'm sure my dad had looked at his teardrop-shaped son during that short, glorious campaign against Saddam Hussein and tried to imagine me commanding a tank, a boy who openly sobbed in the movie theater when 800-year-old Jedi Master Yoda, a green foam latex puppet, quietly died in *Return of the Jedi*, the final movie in the original Star Wars trilogy. Loved Yoda, I did.

He knew I was "sensitive."

My counteroffer was that I apply to an affordable state school with an excellent theatre program and audition. I had the blessing of Mr. Boyd. When I said his name, my mom softly mumbled "bueno" under her breath. She liked Mr. Boyd, even though they were very different people. He was one of the only teachers of color at my public school, which was so white, in fact, that I managed to pass Spanish only because my mom came in and spoke to my teacher *en español*. My hometown was twenty minutes outside of D.C., but it was still a quiet suburb. Most folks in McLean were welcoming and friendly, but there's a reason Confederate General Robert E. Lee's fighting force was called the Army of Northern Virginia.

I told my dad that not only was the school affordable, but it would also likely accept an enthusiastic boy like yours truly whose academic record was mediocre at best. Theatre schools don't care that you have a D in Algebra. So long as Mr. Boyd gave me a glowing recommendation and I nailed the audition, I was sure to get in.

He asked me why I wanted to study theatre, and I gave him a carefully considered answer: Theatre taught the values of hard work, collaboration, and creativity, and those were all valuable skills to have in any profession. I also suggested that it was in the blood. My dad's father, my granddad, was a Baptist preacher, which is a theatre kid for Jesus.

I told him the plan was to learn everything I could about theatre and then get a respectful job when I graduated, one that would recognize my ability to work within a team. My dad grumbled something about the postal service, a stable profession with great benefits and pension. You get to work outside and wear shorts in the summer. It's a solid fallback career.

What I didn't tell him was that I loved wearing makeup. That during the past few years I was learning things about myself that I hadn't known. I loved holding hands with a cast backstage before a performance around a candle and telling each other to break a leg, how much we would miss each other, and that we'd always love one another forever and ever. I didn't tell my dad that I was hooked on make-believe, laughter, and applause, that the friends I made in the theatre department were *mi familia*. I felt safe with them, and when we'd hug, we'd hug with all our might, pressing our bodies against each other, and sometimes those hugs would linger.

I wanted him to know I loved playwrights, language, and stories, that wearing different skins and borrowing voices and feeling feelings for a few hours felt as good as anything I had ever felt.

When I announced my plan, I could see her slowly nod her head as she grated a huge block of orange cheese. She didn't say anything, but I knew what she was thinking. My mom had an "old Mexican saying" for every parental situation. But her favorite was probably "Do you know how to make God laugh?" The punchline was "Make a plan."

She just wanted me to be realistic. Sometimes plans don't work out. Sometimes, you're the butt of God's jokes because God gets bored.

* * *

My mom understood me, or we understood each other. From the moment I could waddle and babble, we'd spend entire weekends strolling through musty thrift store aisles looking for treasures, and while we never found an antique vase that would pay my college tuition, we almost always left carrying armfuls of books.

She was drawn to the great men of Western literature, like Dickens, Faulkner, and Poe. The first book she ever gave me was her copy of Emerson's collected essays, a volume decorated with underlined words and notes in the margins. My mom had never finished college, but she lived a creative life, painting and teaching and, of course, making a home for her family. She was connected to Mexican artists, but it was exotic white men like Thoreau and Whitman, pale and untouched by the cruel Texas sun, that she was drawn to, with their gentle but firm beliefs in individuality.

I was also drawn to these writers, many of whom were raging alcoholics. Eventually, I would find my own literary heroes and learn all the wrong lessons from them. She had bohemian dreams, and I think it pleased her to imagine me filling notebooks with poems at New York City cafes.

She knew I was a natural-born ham before I ever did. There was plenty of evidence. When I was barely seven or eight I'd dance in my underwear to the heroic theme song of the sci-fi TV show *Buck Rogers in the 25th Century*, which featured a muscular man and a foxy woman in tight-fitting, futuristic white spacesuits shooting laser guns. She'd watch me spin and leap and conduct the show's stirring melody. There was also the time when a nun told us during CCD—which was like after-school boot camp for little Catholics—to imagine Jesus's suffering, the nails in his hands, and the blood surging forth. Later that night, I pricked the palms of my hands with thumbtacks and rehearsed dying, noisily, on the cross.

My old man never openly disapproved of Catholicism—he respected my mom too much—but I could tell he wasn't moved by the ancient ritual of Mass, with its incense and gold chalices and robes, a solemn hour-long performance revered by grandmas. The Baptists are raised to make a joyful noise, to sing and sing loud, and Catholics mumble their hymns as if they're sick.

My siblings also knew I was showpeople, both my brothers and my older sister, who used to terrorize me with tickle attacks one moment and then surprise me with mixtapes full of hard-rock classics. They knew I was different; they saw me pose in the bathroom mirror, eyes wide. They loved me anyway.

So it wasn't a surprise when I was cast in my fourth-grade class's production of *The Phantom Tollbooth*, an adaptation of Norton Juster's 1961 children's book of the same name, with illustrations by Jules Ffeifer. It is a fantasy about a bored boy named Milo who is transported to a magical realm of allegorical kingdoms dedicated to language and arithmetic. During his adventures, Milo learns the value of curiosity and imagination. The novel and the play are educational and entertaining, brimming with clever wordplay that I did not understand.

At first, I wasn't interested in being in a play, but then I learned that performing is a way to hide in plain sight. I had one line in one scene. I was cast as a member of story-loving King Azaz's court, and during a feast I was supposed to say to a confused and overwhelmed Milo, "Why not wait for your just desserts?" Only I didn't understand that some characters spoke in idioms and that "just desserts" meant "what you deserve," and no one explained that to me, not even the young, eager director who was brought in to herd a bunch of ten-year-olds and put on a show in a large cafeteria.

So, during rehearsal, I rewrote my line to my satisfaction: "Why don't you just have dessert?" I said that to giggles from my peers. The director quickly corrected me and told me to make sure my line was memorized for the performance and to recite it exactly as it was written. I disobeyed her, of course, and after I delivered my version of the line, I shrugged and mugged, and the entire audience of parents and students erupted into laughter. There was nothing the director could do either, and at that moment, I understood the power of the theatre. It was alive. It wiggled. Fluttered. Television was a beautiful butterfly pithed and pinned, but theatre flaps its wings when released and flies away in whatever direction it wants. Theatre breathes. In and out. It is here one moment and gone the next, forever.

The director was frustrated with my rebellion, and so was my teacher, who told me this was why I wasn't invited into my school's gifted and talented program. She thought that would make me behave, the idea that if I did what I was told, I'd gain entry to the fancy classroom with the best art supplies and a computer in the corner. At my school, in the '80s, there were children deemed worthy of investment, and there was everyone else.

My mom wasn't proud that I hadn't done what I was told but when I told her what the teacher said, she replied, "The gifted and talented class is where they teach you how to be gifted and talented. You already are, mijo."

* * *

He chewed on his cigar for the entire two-hour drive from McLean, Virginia, to my college audition in Richmond. It was the spring of '92 and the radio was nothing but Sir-Mix-a-Lot's irreverent hip-hop hit "Baby Got Back" and right-wing hate potato Rush Limbaugh, and we listened to Rush because my dad wanted to know what the enemy was thinking and saying.

I knew my plan made him uneasy, but the man supported me. Not right at first. Eventually. He tried one more time to influence me, pitching Baylor University in Texas, which was famously affiliated with the Baptist Church and had a drama department, but he quickly gave up after watching my face melt. Later, he told me he talked to a friend on Capitol Hill who knew a Wall Street guy with a theatre degree. He turned out fine, he's rich, college is college.

He dropped me off at Virginia Commonwealth University's campus and shouted "Break a leg!" as I slammed the car door. For the audition, I chose one of Roy Cohn's monologues from Tony Kushner's *Angels in America*, a play that baffled me and hit me right in the heart. Kushner's sprawling, terrifying, uplifting drama about humans in love during a horrible plague moved me in ways I couldn't explain.

I performed the role of a vile, deeply closeted fifty-nine-year-old right-wing monster dying of AIDS with the confidence of a sheltered seventeen-year-old suburban straight boy. I gave a deeply offensive performance—I was stereotypically gay and Jewish and evil, all at the same time. But I gave it my all, and a few months later, I was accepted into the program. It would be the only college acceptance I would receive.

On the drive home from the audition, I was all smiles, which made my dad smile. He smiled and smoked, and we both laughed about this and that and plotted a celebratory Chinese-food takeout feast. We were both passionate about crab rangoon, cream-cheese-filled fried wontons scientifically designed to appeal to American tastes.

It's not like my old man and I had nothing in common. I tried to care about football. If I had been born in Texas, I would probably worship the sport. Texans love football the way the ancient Romans loved crucifixion. But, alas, when I watch football, I see SUV-sized hulks with brain damage using their skulls as battering rams as millions cheer. As for video games, I have never understood the allure. He'd tell me, on many occasions, that most kids would kill for a dad who was into *The Legend of Zelda*.

But we loved crab rangoon! And we were both really into professional wrestling for a few years. He met my mom at a *lucha libre* match in Juarez when he was a part-time ring announcer, and she was a young woman who went to watch the colorful masked *luchadores* fly off the ropes with her father. This was the family origin story. He never connected my theatre obsession with the hours he and I spent watching fabulous he-men bodyslamming each other in a choreographed morality play that was one part rodeo, one part ballet. It's why I loved capes.

We booed the heels and cheered the faces together, but not for long. I never watched a Super Bowl with him, but I sat through more than one WrestleMania, pumping my fist for Randy "Macho Man" Savage and George "The Animal" Steele. But then musicals like *Les Miz* stole my heart, and that was that.

We also told jokes. He loved jokes. Especially lightly inappropriate ones, since he was the son of a preacher man. One of his favorites went like this: A man gets a flat tire outside an insane asylum. A chain-link fence surrounds the asylum, and inside that fence, various patients wander. His predicament catches the attention of one of the patients. The man doesn't like being watched but gets to work changing the tire, placing each lug nut from the flat into its hubcap, which he lays on the street. He can feel the patient watching him and, distracted, accidentally kicks the hubcap, and all the lug nuts spill onto the asphalt and roll down a storm drain. The man is distraught.

So the patient goes, "Look, all you have to do is take one lug nut off of each of the other three tires and use them to put the spare on. That'll get you down the road to a filling station."

The man is shocked and relieved. He can't believe it. What a great idea.

"Look," says the patient, "I'm crazy, not stupid."

That one always made him chuckle, and he told it often. Politics is a serious business—too serious—but he took every opportunity to tell a zinger. He wasn't a clown, which I think is a perfectly acceptable thing to be. He just loved to make other people laugh. He was the type of man who would stop important people in the marble hallways of Washington, D.C. to tell them the one about the guy with the wooden eye or the one about the one-legged woman. The ability to tell a joke, to put strangers at ease, and to make friends, is an important skill if you didn't grow up around money.

He used to ask people he was meeting for the first time whether or not they'd like "my card" and then he would hand them a business card with the words "My Card" printed on them. He had these made specially.

I once asked him the secret to success. He was a press secretary, an important staff position, and he was good at his job. I didn't know that then. I had no idea what he did, actually, except that he left for work at six in the morning with a briefcase, every weekday and sometimes Saturday, and had a small office in the massive, modernist Hart Senate Office Building. I remember being slightly embarrassed that my dad was a secretary, but I knew he had worked for many powerful and wealthy people. How did all those cabinet officials and senators and ambassadors get to where they were? Did he know how they did it? He had met the president before? How did these people become so successful? He paused thoughtfully and told me the secret was equal parts crippling insecurity and backstabbing ambition feeding on each other.

Not long after sharing that observation with me, he gave me the only piece of professional advice he ever offered up. It came out of nowhere and I assumed it represented the sum of his experiences toiling on Capitol Hill. He told me to always return the calls of friends and colleagues who get fired, or laid off, or lose the big election. Everyone stumbles. He said no one calls you when you're down, except the people who care about you.

＊ ＊ ＊

I learned two things about myself in college: I could drink appalling quantities of alcohol, and, more importantly, I was a lousy actor.

Before I left for college my mom told me that I was now old enough to make my own decisions, and so I made my own decisions. One of the first decisions I made was to Just Say Yes to drugs and alcohol. I spent my teenage years scared of the stuff, but all it took was a dorm room full of pimply bros chanting "Drink! Drink!" and one glug of whiskey from a bottle and I was a free man.

I started smoking too. I didn't even cough the first time I lit up. I was a natural. Sophisticated and world-weary. I taught myself to talk while a burning Newport dangled from my lip.

The alcohol did to my anxieties what paint thinner does to oil brushes. I felt lighter and braver and could talk, sing, and dance. I could also be mean and selfish and not care whose feelings I hurt. Thanks to the liquor, I learned how to disappear, and the secret was ice and vodka.

This was a latent ability. When I was ten, my older sister had been in a terrible car accident, and she spent weeks in the hospital. It wrecked the family. But during that ordeal, I would stand very still with my back flat against hospital walls and try to become the wall. I tried so hard. But when I was drunk, all I had to do was close my eyes and nothing mattered. If I couldn't be seen, then I was not responsible for anything, or anyone, including myself.

In the fragrant men's dorms, I met guys like me, my age, from nameless suburbs, who spoke a language I was fluent in: the gender norms of '80s action movies. *Commando. Rambo. Invasion U.S.A.* The macho one-man-army classics. I knew jack about the NFL, but I was a Chuck Norris expert.

To me, at least, action movies were testosterone-juiced musicals where the muscle-bound hero breaks legs instead of breaking into song. These flicks were straight, white, and male and sold the idea that masculinity was a life-long endurance test—that to be a real man, one must absorb pain without complaining.

I quickly learned that while I was physically feeble in many ways, my ability to damage my liver earned me the respect of non–theatre kids, namely frat boys and jocks and other assorted shitkickers who were shocked by my willingness to guzzle Jägermeister like it was fruit punch.

During my Intro to Acting class, I was told that every actor should know their type: handsome lead or weird-looking character actor. Those were the choices. Skinny or chubby, and I was already the latter. I had never really wondered what my "type" was, but I had entered the adult world, and if I didn't categorize myself, someone else would. I was a white man, first and foremost, even though I had checked both "white" and "Hispanic" on my college application.

I know normal people want to think alcoholics have origin stories, but they're not supervillains. They're born, like theatre kids. It's not a choice; there's no "a-ha" moment. Just one day, if you're lucky, you suddenly ask yourself why you're puking your guts up into a public trash can on a crisp Sunday morning.

I didn't know I had a problem. Not back then. I was doing what I thought I should be doing. I was under the impression that true, serious artists with integrity like Jack Kerouac were (a) men and (b) indolent, and (c) desirous of everything simultaneously. This was much more romantic than the bright, cold truth that I was a scared and selfish boy who smelled faintly like bottom-shelf cocktails.

My old man would have one drink with dinner, a gin and tonic, and only at restaurants, which we ate at once or twice a month. I only saw him drunk once, a year or so before he died, after brutal surgery to remove a tumor-riddled lung. He was lit on vodka, clearly self-medicating, and it terrified me to watch him crack jokes while in terrible pain. I wasn't raised by out-of-control alcoholics, and yet I grew up to be one. This happens. The reverse is also true—the children of out-of-control alcoholics can grow up to become gentle, understanding, and responsible adults.

Despite my recently discovered talents for substance abuse, I managed to earn myself the nickname "Narc," given to me by my classmates. It was a joke firmly grounded in the reality that I looked like a middle-aged normie even as an eighteen-year-old. I was typecast.

My fashion sense was, and has always been, inexplicably conservative, and I suppose that was my mom's doing. She wanted me to be an artist, to express myself, but she also dressed me like a little Republican, and in that contradiction lived her wish for me, I suppose, to be daring and safe simultaneously. My haircut in college was best described as "assistant bank manager chic," and even when I abandoned slacks and button-downs for funkier clothes like tie-dyed T-shirts, I still didn't look quite right. It is challenging to buy drugs off the street while resembling an FBI agent.

I wanted to dress like a badass, but I could never pull it off. Body art and modifications were all the rage in the mid-'90s and one of my college girlfriends, Sam, the wild-child daughter of U.S. diplomats, earned cash on the side piercing literally any body part brought to her. Nipples, tongues, bellybuttons. Sometimes her clients bled all over the rug; sometimes they'd pass out. She had a strong stomach, which you had to have if you were raised Mormon, which she was. I must have watched her punch dozens of holes in people. And even then, I never got any ink or perforated my skin in any way, but I did, briefly, have a goatee. Sam hated that. She said it made me look like bewhiskered Evil Spock, from that classic *Star Trek* episode where Captain Kirk finds himself trapped in an alternate reality.

* * *

Theatre school was, mostly, a fun eight semesters of gratuitous carousing, vapid self-expression, and academic underachievement. While other friends of mine studied normal things like history and psychology and took classes with homework, I studied, you know, my feelings. I had vast stockpiles of feelings.

I spent most of the first year of college eating LSD and wandering the streets of Richmond, Virginia, a sleepy Southern city that lounges on the wide, brown James River. I used to stroll around that city past midnight like I was king of the rednecks until I was mugged. I was pistol-whipped and told to get on the ground, and I had no money, so they stole my shoes. I have looked over my shoulder ever since.

Richmond was famous for three things when I lived there, including the shock-metal band Gwar's gory live shows and the headquarters of Philip Morris, makers of Marlboro cigarettes. But it was mostly known as the defeated capital of the Confederacy, and the city never quite got over that loss. Richmond was a city of magnificent avenues and falling-apart row houses, and drugs were easy to find. The statues of fallen Confederate war heroes were still everywhere in the '90s, noble men with beards on horseback. These were monuments to slave masters, built by their racist children and grandchildren: firm reminders that the South would rise again. (It hasn't yet.)

I once laid in the grass underneath Robert E. Lee's statue, stoned, and imagined a fairy tale about these losers coming back to life for a night. Stewart, Jackson, and Lee climbing off their steeds and walking around the city and watching all kinds of different people living together and loving each other, and then returning to their horses with a defeated groan before turning back to bronze.

My class load had very little work. Instead of learning another language, for instance, I studied dialects. I may not know how to speak Italian, but I-a know-a how-a to-a speak-a in-a Italiano accent.

I took an Intro to Playwrighting class with other aspiring control freaks. The student teachers in Set Construction forbade me from using power tools so I spent a lot of time sweeping up the shop. My final exam for Costume Design fell apart once the button met the buttonhole. I even took a contact improv movement class with actual dance majors, who taught me how to keep a straight face if I accidentally farted during a performance.

And, of course, I studied acting. Acting is the art of pretending to be someone else. It can be a very simple or highly complex craft to practice. The best actors in my program were comfortable in their skin, a talent that confounded me. The best actors were also disciplined, and they believed in themselves. They weren't always the most book-smart, but they were wise. They knew themselves and had an innate ability to relax and exist while being stared at. This can't be taught. But that has never stopped anyone from trying.

The problem is that theatre schools can be expensive, and you must get your money's worth. And that's where acting theories come in. My professors were especially enamored of the great Russian director and teacher Konstantin Stanislavski. You may not know Stanislavski's name, but his pioneering acting theories have directly and indirectly influenced generations of theatre artists and even Hollywood itself. He was the first to insist that acting training was more than having good posture and memorizing lines. Acting was an art, after all. He wanted more "naturalistic" performances. "Stan the Man," as one of my professors called him, combined nineteenth-century psychology, script analysis, and good old-fashioned bullshit into a method that churned out dedicated actors.

I found the many details of his acting theories to be impenetrable. The goal was authentic, realistic performances, but the path involved too much chin-stroking for me. I was also frustrated because many classmates turned into Stanislavski experts overnight. The Russian intellectual wanted actors to use their memories and imagination to become their characters fully, but I knew peers who grossly misunderstood that. They wanted to believe their art was alchemical, and my program didn't discourage such romanticism.

Stanislavski wanted his actors to plumb the depths of their inner lives to fuel their performances. Like to cry on stage, I should dig up memories of my dead dog. Of course, an actor does not, and never does, actually become somebody else. Oh, no, no. That would be, you know, crazy.

Legend has it that a disciple of one of the department's acting professors—a working actor—once called his mentor late at night because he was trapped inside his character. That is what I was told secondhand, that he said that verbatim. The poor guy was in some regional show where his character met with a tragic end. Probably some weepy mid-century drama about the fall of the common man. He sobbed that he couldn't shake his role. The character was destroyed at the end of the play, and so was he.

This story was told to me by actors who seemed to marvel at this actor's artistry, and all I could think was, "Fuck, this guy needs help."

* * *

To say I didn't take my acting program by storm is an understatement. My first role in a school production was the stern Duke Theseus in *A Midsummer Night's Dream*, and then . . . nothing. A few background roles, but no lines. So I showed up for a few rehearsals stoned—so what? So I resented not being cast more, or at all. The word got out that I was a pain in the ass and I thought being a pain in the ass was the artist's prerogative.

I had found something I was good at—carousing—and I became less interested in school. I was too busy embalming myself to care. One of the great mistakes of my life has been confusing integrity with fear. I thought I was some kind of *enfant terrible* when, in fact, I was simply a scared little *enfant*.

Ironically, the most academically rigorous class I took was my favorite, Theatre History, which I enjoyed whenever I bothered to attend. I was busy living the life of a poet, which meant I was rarely in class, and when I was, I was nursing debilitating hangovers. I once went to class with a head full of cough syrup, which was a cheap way to get high. For a while there, it was my preferred way to hallucinate. I'd guzzle a couple of bottles of Robitussin and boom! I'd end up in the strangest, most unexpected places, like Theatre History class. I remember one particular lesson. I held it in my hands like a firefly.

It was a brief lesson on the word "theatre," which derives from the Greek *theatron*, or "place of seeing," roughly translated. Whoa. The first theater was, likely, a crackling fire where an elder acted out the day's hunt, begged the gods for rain, or praised their mercy. Theatre and religion are twins, born at the same time. They are rituals that nourish hearts and souls and connect humans. A theater is a church with a stripper pole, where people gather and breathe and sweat, a sacred meeting hall or classroom or basement where one can look at another person and say, "Once upon a time. . . ."

I remember exactly three dates from theatre history: 1967, 1593, and 407 BCE. The British playwright Joe Orton was murdered by his lover Kenneth Halliwell with a hammer in the apartment they shared in 1967. Orton's plays were well-structured drawing-room comedies full of dark humor and sexual innuendo. He was a prankster who would slyly shock proper folk with some of the smartest genital jokes in the English-speaking world.

There isn't a conservatory or regional theater or high school drama department that doesn't worship Shakespeare, and for a time, I considered building my entire personality around hating on the Bard. I was drawn to his frenemy, Kit Marlowe, playwright and spy and all-around rad dude whose great work, *Doctor Faustus*, speaks to dumb young men who will do anything for power and sex. The play is straightforward and lacks Will's linguistic flourishes or a deep sense of humanity's complexities, but it's a great ride. Faustus is a dick, and every young actor is a dick. Marlowe was stabbed to death in 1593 while arguing over a bill.

I had one professor who revered Euripedes, the youngest of the three great Greek tragedians: himself, Sophocles, and Aeschylus. This professor directed a production of Euripedes's *The Trojan Women*, one of the greatest anti-war works of art of all time, a grim coda to the siege of Troy that depicts what happens to all the women who survive Agamemnon's fury.

The professor, a gentlemanly geezer with a constant leer, repeated the myth that Euripedes was killed by wolves one night in 406 BCE, returning from a party. That's probably not true, but I've always liked it. Two years before his death, Euripides wrote his great tragedy, *The Bacchae*, after leaving Greece in a huff for the court of King Archelaus of Macedonia. Euripedes was a celebrity but a cranky, combative one, and history suggests Athens didn't beg him to stay. Most likely, he died an old man from being an asshole.

The Bacchae is a play about Dionysus, the Greek god of wine, and religion, and theatre, and most of all, abandon. Dionysus was the god of getting drunk and dancing and open-mouth kissing. The play is a complex and provocative work about the war between reason and passion, and it ends poorly for the killjoy mortal king Pentheus, who is violently torn apart by Dionysus's orgiastic followers, a group of female worshippers overcome with lust and love.

I wrote a play during that time inspired by *The Bacchae*. I called it *Tupperware Orgy*, and I replaced the wine with LSD and Dionysus with a serial killer. Americans are both terrified of and fascinated by serial killers because they do whatever fucked-up shit they want, and Americans deeply want that kind of freedom. There was an ignorant and arrogant part of me—quite a large slice of my personality if we're being honest here—that thought *Tupperware Orgy* was commercial and I honestly thought, "This will make me lots of money." That was the plan, remember? That is everyone's plan when they're young and scared and dumb.

I once told my plan to a graduate student named Linda, a regal, silver-haired stoner from England. Her voice was melodic and commanding. She was an actress and a scholar—a mother of two older sons—and her humble apartment was a crumbling ruin of books. I once read her a love poem I had composed for someone I was pining over, a wretched chunk of sappy free verse. Linda regarded it kindly and admitted she had once written a love poem to a girlfriend too.

She'd make me tea, and we'd have intense philosophical conversations. "Conversations" is a generous word for them. I'd sit there and listen to her quietly preach about her favorite topics. Art. Bliss. The Occult. I'd ask her heartfelt questions like, "What do I do?" And she'd pull a tarot card and whisper, "Do what thou wilt."

So I did.

I partied. I barely went to class. I put in the bare minimum. I looked down on my professors. I thought they were all sell-outs who couldn't "make it" in showbiz.

The faculty was a motley crew of academics and professionals making a little side cash teaching Virginia's most talented students who couldn't afford out-of-state tuition. I saw them all as spoilsports and scolds and schoolmarms, but that was a failure of my imagination. What I didn't see at the time—what I was incapable of seeing—was adults being paid to play. Teach, yes. But also, they were paid to make theatre. Good gig.

There was the rumpled acting teacher who loved wearing scarves inside and would appear on local TV commercials from time to time and the voice teacher from Boston who loved tongue-twisters but hated cigarettes—It's such a bad habit! It ruins your instrument! Your voice! In fact, most of the faculty despised the habit, save for the head of the department, a graceful, gravel-voiced imp who sucked death sticks all day long. More than one professor would recoil in mock disgust whenever they'd smell cigarettes on my clothes, or see me puffing away outside in the cold.

The GI Bill had paid for the educations of some of the older professors, including a giant of a man who was well-known in Central Virginia for playing a hilariously haughty Mrs. Malaprop in numerous local revivals of Oscar Wilde's comedy of manners *The Importance of Being Earnest*.

To the faculty, I was a basket case who'd come to class inebriated, an arrogant little prick at worst, a doofus at best, and so they made it easy for me to graduate, and one way they did that was by not casting me in any school productions. They just wanted to be rid of me, and this was the easiest way. They even wrote me a formal letter informing me that I was *persona non grata* in the acting department, but they suggested I finish my remaining credits taking creative writing classes, which I did. I would get a BFA. I learned a lot at school despite my all of my efforts to the contrary.

So I acted off-campus. I decided I was going to show them. There were a few small theaters in Richmond, and I tried out for parts here and there. I was almost immediately cast in a touring Purim spiel, a freewheeling comedic sketch about the festive Jewish holiday that celebrated the survival of Mordecai and Esther and God's Chosen living in ancient Persia. The director was a former grad student named Jeff who thought I was funny and was willing to put up with my shit. I wouldn't say Jeff was an optimist, but he was always smiling. He was 60 percent mensch, 40 percent nudnik. In the Purim spiel, I played the villainous Haman's sidekick, Abu, and I was, in a word, wacky. We would show up at nondescript temples all around the Richmond area, and the small rooms we'd perform in would fill with local Jews who laughed at the zany college kids. For a few brief weekends, I was a sex symbol. After each performance, I'd be introduced to someone's nice young daughter and we'd both blush.

And then I was cast in my biggest role—then and now—playing Edgar Allan Poe in a three-hour, interactive, site-specific theatrical experience at the Valentine Art Museum in Richmond.

The show's concept was simple. Each night, the audience was invited to wander the rooms of a "The Masque of the Red Death"–inspired masquerade ball hosted by me, Edgar Allan Poe. In each room, a macabre story like "The Tell-Tale Heart" was acted out, or a poem like "Annabel Lee" performed with amateur recklessness.

At the time, I suspected my acting skills were average, at absolute best. I mean, deep down, I knew. I had spent hours in acting class watching how it was done, and I did not do it as well. But as Poe, I indulged in a little more self-deception than usual. Maybe I was a brilliant actor? What if I had been misunderstood? After all, if I wasn't brilliant, why did the director cast me? The answer to that is that maybe she regretted it. I never asked.

So I raved. Anyone who knew anything about Poe knew he wasn't a raving lunatic. That is a popular stereotype. Edgar Allan Poe was a brilliant, troubled man who led a short, tragic life, but I didn't spend a lot of time researching him.

I knew he was the son of theatre kids, a pair of impoverished actors. An orphan. He invented entirely new literary genres and enjoyed few successes during his forty years of life. He struggled with poverty and the bottle. His relationship with his cruel adoptive father was fraught. Both his mother and young wife, Virginia, died from tuberculosis. When he was a boy, he wit-nessed a cholera outbreak. He knew about pain, and death, and loss. He wrote about pain, and death, and loss. The man always knew America was a nightmare.

Poe grew up in Richmond. This, alone, should be the most important fact about that city. Forget Robert E. Lee and J.E.B. Stuart, there should be an 500-foot-tall bronze statue of Poe in the middle of Richmond. He was born in Boston and died in Baltimore—and both cities lazily lay claim to his legacy—but he considered himself a Richmond native. This is why I wasn't the only Poe impersonator in town.

There was a rumor that Richmond's most famous Poe impersonator was not pleased he had competition. This man dressed like Poe on the weekends. He was older and committed to the role. He had memorized "The Raven"! The whole thing! You could hire him the way you'd hire a birthday clown or magician. Anyway, I was briefly afraid of him. I knew I would lose any Poe-off.

I grew a mustache for the part. My hair was naturally long and wild like the man himself, but my mustache looked like a hairy candy bar. I wore a puffy white shirt and a cape. I also adopted a ridiculous Southern accent, like I was related to Colonel Sanders. Full disclosure: I was drunk during many performances. Obviously. At the time, I thought this was how serious artists made art, and that is not true.

One of my big moments was performing Poe's poetic masterpiece, "The Raven." When he was alive he'd tour the Northeast reciting the gothic poem as a cash-hungry one-hit-wonder has-been. I could never remember the poem so I wrote it down and hid the pages in a large book that looked like a wizard's grimoire. I'd open it slowly and read like I was casting a spell. It's a brilliant poem, of course. Even I couldn't wreck it, but there were nights I came close.

Another actorly duty of mine was occasionally fun. I was supposed to interact with the audience like a historical reenactor at some colonial tourist trap. I'd greet paying customers with an over-the-top "Allow me to intro-duce myself. Mah name is Edgar Allan Poe." Sometimes I acted like a ghost, sometimes I was a man who accidentally stepped through a tear in the fabric of space-time. I enjoyed this because I made up all the lines. I got to improvise from beginning to end, except when I had to recite a Poe poem or a snippet from a short story, and then I'd just read aloud from the book.

As the show reached its climax—hours later—I would disappear and change into a "Red Death" costume. The cast and audience were mixed together in a single crowd by this time. I'd emerge and proceed to touch each cast member, infecting them with Poe's made-up disease. This was their cue to die, horribly and loudly. I'd slowly move from actor to actor, through the crowd, winking at some, whispering plans to meet at the bar to others, but never breaking character.

When they were all dead on the concrete floor of the museum's garden, I would take off my mask and reveal myself to whoever was still there—we always lost people throughout the night who ran for the doors once they realized Poe's works were being reduced to improvisational sketches. I would then, for no good reason, also die horribly and loudly. At first, I'd gurgle, and clutch my throat. Depending on my mood, I'd reach out to an audience member with a hand like a claw, begging them for help as I coughed and crumpled and convulsed. Finally, I'd collapse. There was always a long pause before the audience realized the show was over, and they'd applaud.

And I'd slowly stand up, exhausted. I'd bow and blow kisses. Yes, I was a star. The *Richmond Times-Dispatch* even sent their theatre critic—a real ink-stained wretch—who knew he was reviewing a bunch of college kids and was overly generous to everyone involved except for me, whom he described simply as "strident," a word I did not know at first and hoped was complimentary. I secretly hoped my professors had read the review. I imagined them watching my performance and admitting, with tears in their eyes, that they were wrong about me.

* * *

I moved to New York from Austin, Texas, in the fall of 1996.

My parents had retired to the promised land of the Lone Star State in 1994, and I spent a few months there the summer after I graduated, plotting my next move. They drove me to the airport after weeks of asking me, "Are you sure?"

They escorted me to the gate of the plane I would take to New York's LaGuardia. He pulled me aside and gave me an extra roll of quarters to call home. I told him I had enough quarters, but he was right: you can never have too many quarters. Then he shook my hand and embraced me like I was going off to war. She gave me a long look and hugged me too. She gave me the following advice: keep half of my cash in my shoe in case I got mugged. She also reminded me to be respectful to cops, especially in a big city like New York. Mind your manners. Cops are dangerous. I might be white, she reminded me, but better safe than sorry.

Then she looked me in the eyes and said that if I needed her, I could call her collect from anywhere, anytime, for any reason, and she'd get on a plane. My mom hated flying, but her offer was a one-time deal.

I had a few traveler's checks folded neatly in my wallet, and I stuffed three packs of Marlboro Lights into the pockets of the new winter coat I'd found at a thrift store in Austin. My suitcase was surprisingly light: a few changes of clothes and toiletries, three brand-new black-and-white composition books, and a plastic statue of the Virgin Mary with a screw-top crown that you could pour Holy Water in, or vodka. My mom snuck that one in. She also packed a brand-new tub of the mentholated topical ointment Vick's VapoRub, which she believed remedied everything from aches and sprains to coughs and fevers. It was an ancient Mexican cure-all in my house.

I sat in my seat, fidgeted, and fell into a deep sleep. When I woke up and looked outside my airplane window, I saw the impossible concrete vastness of Manhattan below and immediately started to tremble with anxiety.

The city was full of no-bullshit tough guys—or, at least, that's what I had learned from television—but I was a jelly donut. So I acted like a real hard-ass from the moment I disembarked from the plane: I walked with a slight limp, as if I'd seen shit, and I scowled. My hope was that no one could see I was a jelly donut. When I got into a cab, I immediately told the cabbie to take me to the 23rd Street YMCA, and he could see I was a jelly donut. When I got to the enormous French Renaissance–style YMCA building—which I think was later converted into luxury condominiums—I walked up to the bulletproof glass and said, "My name is John DeVore, and I have a reservation." I paid my fee for the week and found my small, clean room with a single bed, a chest of drawers, and a cold linoleum floor. A shared bathroom was down the hall.

The Y had rented rooms to young men who had traveled to the city in search of their fortune for over a hundred years, a business model they would abandon by the end of the century. This story is not unique; I get it. I am not, nor have I ever been, a special flower. Right now, some kid is getting off a plane at LaGuardia or a bus at Port Authority from some dull state with a head full of outrageous dreams and delusions. I was probably one of who knows how many cherub-faced ding-dongs arriving in New York City on November 4, 1996, just another one of untold millions who believed the gorgeous lie that there's a magical city yonder full of hope and opportunity, a safe space for the ridiculous and the ambitious and the unloved.

I was a nobody who barely knew anybody. But I did know Yvonne, who was one of my best friends from school. I was so relieved that she was in the big city, too, and that we were going to "make it." I just knew we would. Together. She was a tall, slender, wildly talented black woman whose grand-mother had grown up in Germany during the war. Yvonne spoke perfect Deutsch. She was the first biracial person I'd ever really gotten to know.

For most of my life, I was either ashamed of my mom's skin color or angry when some redneck would call her a racial slur out of a car window if she got to a parking space first. I hated that she and I, together, could draw the attention of bored bigots, the sort of dudes who'd tell her to go back to where she came from. ("Texas?")

I remember watching my mom proudly ignore sneers from old white ladies sitting behind cash registers at thrift stores or security guards with crew cuts who would slowly follow her at K-Mart. I was afforded slightly different privileges from my mom, especially as I grew older. The world opens for well-behaved white boys.

At a bookstore in town, I once overheard a few locals ask one another if my mom was Iranian. This wasn't long after the Iran Hostage Crisis, 444 days of near-constant news about terrorists and blindfolded Americans. So, 1982? '83? The rage and fear directed toward Iran and anyone who looked Middle Eastern seeped into everything, including my dreams. I knew better than to say anything to them. My mom made me promise her long ago that I would fight my fights and not worry about hers.

Yvonne knew what it was like to move through the world with a parent who wasn't their color; she knew what it was like to be stared at and judged, and she saw other white people refuse to accept that a white woman could give birth to anyone but another white person. She was a powerful actor, regal and intense. Self-contained. We both bonded over the idea that we were neither this nor that, black or white, Latino or German. She and I shared the same sort of silly sense of humor. We made each other laugh.

Yvonne spent her first few months in the city living at the Catherine House, a dormitory for young adult women under the age of twenty-five. It was inexpensive, maybe a hundred dollars and change a week, but hard to get into. It was a bit like the YMCA where I was staying, only nicer, and stuffier. The rooms were cozier, and there was a cafeteria where the renters could enjoy very basic breakfasts and dinners. There were all kinds of rules, including nightly quiet hours, and the strictest rule was that no boys could visit any rooms at any time for any reason. The women who ran it were Dickensian harridans who thought their job was to protect the virtue of their charges.

I spent a lot of time hanging out with Yvonne in the lobby of the Catherine House. She would sneak me apples and sandwiches from the cafeteria, and on more than one occasion, I fell asleep on the uncomfortable Victorian couches that they kept in the parlor, which is where I imagined gentlemen callers of yore would wait when they came a-callin'.

Yvonne and I spent those weeks sitting in Union Square Park and splitting packs of Marlboro Lights. We'd share black bean nachos at Dojo, an eclectic cheap-eats spot popular with NYU students, or devour a plate of fries at Cozy Diner on 8th Street. Every hour or so, I'd call my answering service from a street payphone to see if a job had materialized, and if it hadn't, we'd move on to another park, Tompkins or Washington Square.

And the whole while, we'd talk about the future. Our future. We'd come up with names for our theatre company and brainstorm our mission statement because half the fun of starting a theatre company is writing a flowery mission statement. We were constantly cold, hungry, and broke, but we were happy.

* * *

My relationship with New York City during those months was volatile, like an illicit affair. We were hot and heavy; sometimes, the city would betray or ignore me. I believed in the famous song with a near-religious fervor: "If I can make it there, I'll make it anywhere." I repeated that line as I walked the sidewalks in the cold, as if I was praying to the God of Concrete and Steel and Brand New Starts. That's the problem with gods, though. Sometimes, they just fuck with you because they can.

I sat on a park bench covered in piss one dispiriting day. I had been looking for work, to no avail. I smelled it the moment I felt the wetness clawing through my jeans. Shortly thereafter, I started coming into contact with more bodily fluids, subway cars splattered with vomit and a glob of semen on the handrail of the stairs of my YMCA. A woman spit at me after I told her I didn't have any money, which was not true. I knew it was all a test, but each time it happened, I used my precious quarters to call home on a payphone to hear my mom's voice and to tell her I was doing great when I was not doing great.

"How are you, mijo?"

I'd breathe deeply and try not to blubber. "I'm having the time of my life."

So I kept at it, filling out endless applications for retail gigs that didn't hire me. I could not get a waiting job to save my life, either. I had no experience and I couldn't name three wines that didn't have screw tops. I looked like I lived in a basement too. And then I applied to a few temp agencies. I bought a tie from a thrift store. I smiled more.

The various managers at the temp jobs I went to were thoroughly unimpressed with me. The mid-luxury fashion showroom didn't like my clothes-folding skills. I operated a freight elevator clumsily. I was a terrible telemarketer. First, the scripts they provided lacked pizazz. I learned that pizazz is not an asset in telemarketing.

I wasn't even selling anything. I was cold-calling numbers ripped from the phone book and asking strangers if they wanted free tickets to the screening of a new TV show. I couldn't even give away something that was free.

But I learned to enjoy temping, for a little while, at least. The word "temp" is short for "temporary." Life is temporary. Temps don't quit; they just disappear in a puff of smoke and reappear at another job elsewhere.

The first temp agency I applied to openly mocked my lack of computer knowledge. I was given two choices: spend my last few hundred dollars on a computer class conveniently taught by the temp agency, or die of hunger. The first day of class was booting up a desktop computer and learning that a screen was called a monitor. Day two was a ballet class of point and click, point and click, point and click. Later, I learned how to copy and paste. Watch this: I learned how to copy and paste.

I asked a fellow classmate what she did when she wasn't pointing and clicking, and she told me she was an intern at a law firm. Oh la-di-da, a law firm. Then she told me all sorts of companies had internships. Foot, meet door. I applied for unpaid positions when I wasn't in class. It was an act of desperation, like a starving cowboy eating his own horse.

Then I got a nibble.

The phone interview consisted of one question: Was I in school? Of course—I was about to start my postgraduate studies in Microsoft Word. Eventually, I'd get a Master's in Microsoft Office. When I learned I had gotten the job that didn't pay, I emotionally ate two potato knishes.

The fact that an internship is a job where you work for free was such an alien concept to me that I failed to comprehend it. The thought couldn't fit in my head. This was my big break. I just pretended to have a new job at a big-time entertainment company.

"Hello, Mom? Dad? I've made it. Please, please, can you Western Union me fifty dollars?"

The internship was with a casting director for Disney who was very friendly and worked long hours. She frequently ate lunch in her office, and I sometimes watched her devour the turkey sandwiches she'd get delivered from the corner deli.

She had an assistant who sat at a desk in what would have been a waiting room. I worked in a chair next to the desk of the assistant to the casting director, and my job was to mostly separate audition headshots into a "yes" pile, a "no" pile, and a "dog" pile, which the assistant told me was the pile for headshots that were laughably pathetic. My desk was my lap.

The office was also shared by the actor Rick Moranis, whose sci-fi comedy *Honey, I Shrunk the Kids* was a huge hit for the Mouse. He was the first bona fide celebrity I had seen in the flesh, and I wanted to know what he knew. I mean, I could quote all his lines from *Ghostbusters*! When we rode the elevator together, he never saw me glance at him because he never noticed me.

I called my mom on a payphone to tell her I was working with the star of one of our favorite musicals, *Little Shop of Horrors*.

It didn't take long to realize that if I hung out near the 50th Street subway stop at 7:50 a.m., I could catch him walking to work wearing a large winter hat with floppy tassels. Sometimes I would walk behind him close enough that I could have walked directly through him if I had been a ghost.

There are better words than "stalked" to describe how I would follow him to work in the morning. I prefer "studied" or "observed, very closely." I didn't tiptoe behind him like a Soviet spy wearing a fake mustache. I just simply walked behind him in a calm and non-threatening way.

We then rode the elevator up to the same floor together.

He would occasionally exit his small office and chat with my boss's assistant—who I thought, at the time, was a real power player in the entertainment industry. She wasn't much older than me, but she was effortlessly cruel toward actors, and I was easily impressed by displays of power, even cheap spectacles like casually mocking desperate glossy black-and-white smiles. The two would whisper-giggle, and I would sit next to her like a pet from space.

It turns out interns don't quit either, but I did anyway.

I needed a job that paid me money, preferably U.S. dollars. I needed rent, food, and toothpaste.

I marched into the casting director's office without knocking and informed her that I was tendering my resignation, effective immediately. She had been eating her lunch but put down her turkey sandwich to give me her full attention. She asked me if I was sure. I said my mind was made up. We shook hands and she wished me luck.

Eventually, a small publishing company hired me to be a receptionist. Being a receptionist fit my skill set: I could answer phones. I could smile. I could answer phones. I was given a break by an editor: I was told to find three typos in that day's edition of *The New York Times* and I found one. He hired me to fact-check a trade magazine about accounting software and laptops called *Small Business Computing Magazine* the very next day. My career was off to a roaring start.

Not long after that, Yvonne would fall in love with an enthusiastic, rubber-faced actor who read my plays and declared them brilliant. He convinced her to move with him to Vancouver, where he was from, and she did. She followed her heart, and took our plans with her.

* * *

I kept in touch with a few others from Richmond who were living in New York. One fellow grad introduced me to a playwright and director named Tuvia, who spoke with a thick Israeli accent. He was gruff and jolly, part Santa Claus, part low-level crime boss. Tuvia wrote sharp comedies about politics and religion. He was a real shit-stirrer, a rabble-rouser. I had never met one. He asked me if I was Jewish, and I said "No," and he gave me his best "nobody's perfect" shrug and cast me in a few readings produced by the Jewish Theater of New York, which he had founded and led as its artistic director.

Once every few weeks, a small group of other Virginia Commonwealth University grads from different years would gather informally, a loose clique of go-getters and overachievers who had put in the work to get their BFAs. I was too good for them, obviously, but I was lonely, and one brisk night, I begrudgingly agreed to meet a few of them at a bar to complain about the exorbitant cost of headshots and the pointlessness of the cattle-call auditions listed in *Backstage*, the theatre trade rag. The most popular grievance was the "you can't get an agent without experience, you can't get experience without an agent" Catch-22, as if agents were magical leprechauns who could abracadabra their clients into winning Tonys. It was like everyone at the bar had the exact same piece to the puzzle of hitting it big in New York City.

During the boozy group therapy session, I met a friend of a friend, a confident actor-slash-singer-slash-dancer-slash-director-slash-phony who had graduated from an excellent school in the Midwest and seemed to know exactly what he was doing. I was immediately drawn to his reckless energy. We were the same age, but I listened to him as if he were a wise and ancient wizard.

The first thing he just blurted out was that self-producing your work was frowned upon in the American theatre unless it was an "industry show-case," where you sang or acted your heart out for agents and producers and other mysterious, nameless members of the "industry." Showcases were desperate and expensive, and the industry never went. He used "industry" and "the American theatre" interchangeably, as if the theatre was one large institution, like the mafia or the DMV, instead of a slowly, constantly dying art form.

This friend of a friend loved musical theatre, and one of his favorite jokes was how you could never catch him south of 14th Street, which was the border separating uptown from the backcountry. Over beer and mozzarella sticks, he explained to me the taxonomy of the American theatre, starting with Broadway, a word that was also short-hand for "success." Broadway was the tippy-top of the theatre-industrial complex, a brutal capitalist battlefield in the heart of Manhattan where forty-one professional theaters competed to produce a hit. The generally accepted belief was that every Broadway season was a collection of dozens of flops, save for two: one would break even, and the other would be such a fabulous smash it would pay for the failures.

To hear him tell tell it, after Broadway came Off-Broadway, which included theaters with one foot in the marketplace and the other in America's strange nonprofit dreamscape, where art was freed from the shackles of capitalism thanks to the generosity of fickle donors and impenetrable state and federal bureaucracies, or that's the idea. Off-Broadway was where more challenging works could be nurtured: quirkier plays instead of bright, sunny musicals. Off-Broadway was too good for Broadway, but it desperately wanted to be Broadway.

He skipped over the primary, practical, differences between the two Broadways, which had to do with size. Broadway included any house with 500 or more seats, and anything between 499 and 100 was Off-Broadway.

Next up were the regional theaters, which, like Off-Broadway venues, were performing arts organizations in big cities like Chicago and Seattle and Washington, D.C., committed to serving their communities, even if those communities were indifferent to the theatre. Regional theatre artistic directors know a lot about what's happening on Broadway.

Then came university theatre departments, the top three being Juilliard, NYU, and the Yale School of Drama. And then there was everything else, including my alma mater, Virginia Commonwealth University, and dropping my school's name probably closed more doors than it opened. After that came dinner theatre, an honest and thankless gig that has helped pay the rents of actors for decades and decades, and community theatre. And by "community theatre," I mean theatre made by actual community members, amateurs whose only ambition is having fun. Maybe you'd be surprised to learn these people usually know very little about what's happening on Broadway.

The cutoff for Off-Broadway venues was 100 seats. What if your New York theater had fewer than that? Then you were an inhabitant of the wasteland known as Off-Off-Broadway. And there's a vast chasm—an abyss, really—separating Broadway, Off-Broadway, regional theatre, and dinner theatre from Off-Off-Broadway, the madwoman in the attic of the theatre world. Experimental! Offensive! Commercially radioactive! They say the neon lights are bright on Broadway, but Off-Off-Broadway was for losers, a backwater populated by uncivilized actors and playwrights who were worse than amateurs. They were wannabes, and it was best to avoid that cursed forest if at all possible; it was full of witches. (This was 100 percent true. Off-Off-Broadway is thick with witches.)

I knew this person was biased, and he had his dreams and plans, and those dreams and plans were to be a working theatremaker. He was full of himself, but his wants were simple. Make theatre, pay the bills. Become the next Mandy Patinkin.

Me? I wanted to be an iconoclast. There's a Sam Shepard quote that goes, "I don't want to be a playwright. I want to be a rock and roll star." Now, Shepard could pull that quote off because of his swagger. He wrote these absurd, grotesque satires and briefly dated Patti Smith, the lanky punk poet and real-life rocker, a living downtown art saint. I was attracted to Shepard's East Village cowboy schtick, and that's what I wanted. To burn. To be loved and feared. To date Patti Smith.

* * *

David took a moment to size me up the first time we talked. Who the hell was this guy? I was a cocky go-getter trying way too hard. He had recently been roped into editing The New York International Fringe Festival's daily newspaper, cheekily and honestly titled *Propaganda*. He needed help producing and distributing each issue and I volunteered. I was qualified, after all. I worked for *Small Business Computing and Communications Magazine*.

David got the unpaid Fringe Festival job because he was already chronicling the downtown scene. He was an actor, but he also the co-founder and editor of a self-published 'zine called *OFF*, which was full of reviews and think pieces about what was important to the Off-Off-Broadway theatre community in the late '90s. When I found this out, I immediately asked him if I could write for *OFF*, too, and he begrudgingly agreed. I don't think David wanted to mentor anyone, but I gave him very little choice in the matter. Eventually, he warmed to my hyperactive charms, once he was certain I wasn't planning on murdering him and assuming his identity.

As a newly minted 'zine critic I was paid in free theatre tickets to shows starring downtown "art stars" like the alt-comedian and playwright Trav SD, a rascally, Groucho-like carnival barker who wore greasepaint glasses and mustache, and The Bindlestiff Family Cirkus, a vibrant neo-vaudeville troupe full of tattooed burlesque dancers, contortionists, fire-eaters—real sexy, demonic sideshow stuff. There were these snarky anti-poetry slams I'd go to hosted by a performance artist wearing plastic elf ears, and I thought she was the coolest person I'd ever seen. I was also drawn to and slightly terrified by Reverend Billy of the Church of Stop Shopping, an activist/performance artist who preached against the evils of capitalism.

It was around this time I heard the story of a writer-director who would sleep on the basement floor of a tiny, dirty ground-floor Off-Off-Broadway theater, his pallet surrounded by a homemade chicken-wire fence he built to keep the rats away from him while he slept. He was that dedicated to his art. I wanted to be that dedicated to my art too.

Each issue of *OFF* was printed with smearable ink on tissue-thin newspaper and hand-delivered across town, to hipster cafes like The Pink Pony on Stanton Street, and to the lobbies of established downtown theaters like HERE, which had been producing offbeat performance art since 1993.

I looked up to David, partly because he was a version of the sort of person I wanted to be. He was a product of the bleak, wintry no man's land that is New Hampshire, a stoney-faced New Englander who craved emotion and warmth. He was also educated in a way that I envied. He could quote classics, he had read Goethe and Shaw and Suzan-Lori Parks and could talk for hours about the work of avant-garde theatre directors like Robert Wilson or Elizabeth LeCompte.

David was a member in good standing of New York's experimental theatre scene, having toured with Richard Foreman in one of his bizarro spectacles and being a friend and collaborator of Assurbanipal Babilla, a stocky, muscular, fiftysomething Iranian performance artist with a wild bushy mustache who had barely escaped his country's right-wing religious revolution. Bani, as he was known (it rhymed with Franny), was famous in his country for wild, erotic, deeply Christian, and extremely gay work, and David was his protégé.

Bani, at his peak, when I first met him, resembled a cross between the great actor Omar Sharif and Super Mario. He had a compact potbelly and twinkling eyes and spoke with an exotic, sing-songy accent that sounded Middle Eastern, English, and Italian all at once. He would stretch certain vowels for fun, and he'd punctuate every sentence with a mischievous smile, like a Persian Cheshire cat. He was fond of calling his friends "Baby," a word he would slowly pull apart. Baaaaabeeeee.

David had directed a one-man show that was written and performed by Bani at the Kraine Theater on 4th Street. He invited me to see it, and I accepted. That was the first time I ever saw Bani—I had heard about him, of course. He stalked the stage while drawing deeply on a cigarette during the preshow as the audience found their seats, and he made direct eye contact with whoever dared. This was the only time he was ever clean-shaven in my memory, and he was handsome.

The play was called *Something Something Über Alles*. It was a long, serpentine monologue about a man cursed and blessed with an uncanny resemblance to Adolf Hitler and an underground cult of hedonistic Hitler worshippers who discover him and offer to fulfill his heart's darkest desires. It is a play about religious ecstasy and the flesh and the nature of evil. Bani was captivating, powerful, and vulnerable; he could pivot from earthy clown to pathetic wretch effortlessly, making you laugh and swoon one moment, then recoil with fear the next.

There is a fleeting moment in any great work of theatre when you're not sitting in a theater watching actors on a stage anymore; you're somewhere else, another reality, a softer, more intense one, and you are filled with light and you gasp. A bad play feels like your brain is slowly turning into cold oatmeal, but a good play? You float. *Something Something Über Alles* builds in sexual fury as the story of the main character becomes a story of human sacrifice, and in the last few seconds, Bani made a sudden and terrifying physical transformation and he became small, and fragile and scared. I floated. I gasped.

Afterward, I was speechless. Bani accepted my praise playfully, and David listened to my analysis of what I had seen. He had become, to me, my professor in an unaccredited downtown New York theatre MFA program. It was cheaper than the real thing. Sometimes he'd get free tickets to a show because he'd offer to review it in *OFF*, and sometimes we'd cough up the ten bucks and just go see whatever was at the Red Room or Soho Rep. I saw so much work with him, weird and abstract installations and movement pieces that were not interested in linear narratives but probed their audiences' psyches in search of undiscovered nerve endings to pluck like fiddle strings, and it was in these performances that my idea of what a story was expanded.

I was raised on sitcoms, and movies and beginnings and endings and heroes and villains, and Off-Off-Broadway was a twilight zone that didn't care about anything most Americans cared about. It was a loose network of empty spaces filled with dreams that never end and stories where nothing happens, and the boy does not get the girl and boys and girls don't exist, there are only flesh-and-blood humans with painted faces screaming, crying, climbing over the audience.

We'd stride into theaters like the legendary Cherry Lane Theater and Theatre for the New City or deep into Brooklyn to warehouses or apartments or wherever the city's brightest and strangest convened to try to make sense of it all and the "it" could be sex or money or gender or politics or beauty.

There were monotone monologists and theatre companies who would spend months workshopping a play about something random, like an umbrella or an old-fashioned bicycle or a postcard bought at a flea market.

He'd drag me to anything downtown that was fresh and new: anarchist cabarets in the West Village, chaotic midnight burlesque shows, and gentle-man zombies reading pornographic poems in parking lots. That sort of stuff. By my calculations, we sat through approximately 10,000 theatrical happenings that were each dramatically illuminated by only one bare light bulb.

Those were years rich with nudity too. Predominantly male. Stage nudity was shocking once, but by the late '90s, it was *de rigueur*. Even the squares yawned at the sight of penises. I saw many and they were rarely erotic. There was one show I remember where penises were twisted like animal balloons.

David and I were especially judgemental when it came to the Bard. We saw so much Shakespeare, much of it forgettable or a punishing mix of pre-tentious and sluggish. Sometimes we were surprised: a bare-bones *Othello* performed in a parking lot south of Houston Street, a rollicking, high-concept *A Midsummer's Night Dream* set in a disco. There was this one guy who would perform a one-person *Macbeth* but with action figures. Ninja action figures. He was funny.

The experimental performances we'd see were nonlinear and defied meaning and moral instruction. These were experiences, like getting lost in a snowstorm. Then we'd talk. It seemed like David had read and seen every-thing, but he never made me feel like I didn't know anything. I knew how I felt and I'd comment on my feelings and that was enough. This play made me feel sad and this play made me feel like the moon. Americans like art with a function, like a screwdriver or a blender. But in Off-Off-Broadway, art could be a fish, or a shoe. What does this play say? It says, "Fuck you."

We made it a habit of leaving the very nanosecond the house lights went up, and we'd spill out into the street laughing or mock-sobbing or, usually, discussing what we liked and what we hated, each of us trying to one-up the other with a witty observation or one-liner, like younger versions of Waldorf and Statler, the cantankerous old coots who live to heckle Kermit the Frog and friends from the safety of their balcony in *The Muppet Show*.

You know, the Beckettian geezers who sing the lyrics "Why do we always come here / I guess we'll never know / It's like a kind of torture / To have to watch the show."

We both loved the romantic idea that a play could change the world, and we both loved talking to actresses and drinking in bars and livin' la vida loca, and there were times I'd bang on the bathroom stall to see if he'd stopped puking, and there were times when he'd return the favor. And then there were nights when the lights would fall at Collective:Unconscious or Expanded Arts, and I would applaud because I was stunned or shocked, and then David and I would float out of the theater, our conversations fueled by enthusiasm and inspiration and I'd have an idea, or he'd have an idea, and the idea would be "Let's go to Kokie's," the cocaine speakeasy in Williamsburg that sold cheap, low-quality drugs in a Spartan and unfriendly environment.

* * *

I had discovered the Fringe thanks to *The Village Voice*, an alternative weekly newspaper that would appear in massive bales all over New York City on Tuesday nights, and the paper was full of left-wing editorials and sex advice and the best damn horoscopes in the business, and in the back of those newspapers were listings for apartments and jobs, and reviews of plays and dance pieces and strange works of art, and I would read that newspaper in my cold studio apartment in Queens. There were also ads for massages. Lots of ads for massages. Massages at any hour of the day or night.

I learned about New York City's lower depths in *The Village Voice*. The goody-goodies uptown read *The New York Times* but the vampires read the

Voice. It was my primary downtown cultural textbook. The first time I had ever read about Mabou Mines or Elevator Repair Service was in that newspaper. Those theatre companies were hell-bent on making art on their terms. That was the goal. If you didn't "get it" then you didn't "get it," and I wanted to get it.

My next step was to get involved, so I reached out to the most connected person I personally knew. I became part of the Fringe thanks to Sandi, a writer and actor I had met on the set of an independent movie in Boston that we were both cast in the summer right after I graduated college.

It had been a screwball comedy titled *Starving Artists*, written, directed, and starring a high school friend of mine, Allan. He had a booming voice, a corny sense of humor, and a sincere affection for me, which always made me cringe. Why me? I spent most of high school trying to avoid Allan because his friendship was so pure and freely given. He went to Harvard, and I visited him there one semester. I was trashed on the train from Richmond up north. One of my few claims to fame was introducing the Harvard Glee Club to malt liquor.

He wrote me a funny part in his movie; I was the wacky roommate. I was paid nothing but I ate for free.

Sandi had befriended me during the shoot with a nonchalant nod. Months later, we both moved to New York City and had coffee on the Lower East Side. She was a natural on camera, effortless and honest, and she knew all sorts of folks because she was the sort that others, including me, gravitated toward. They say it's not what you know, it's who you know, and in the summer of 1997, I knew Sandi, and she vouched for me.

She dragged me to a meeting for the second New York International Fringe Festival. I was nervous. The room was crowded with art-school lowlifes, and I shook the hand of one of the Fringe's founders, a handsome, roguish actor who reminded me of a cross between Han Solo and Bertolt Brecht. He was a born bullshit artist too. But he was married to a warm, funny actor who was both motherly and intimidating. She was the better half, that was clear. It was after that meeting that I'd met David.

FringeNYC, for short, was a two-week circus of high-concept, DIY-meets-MTV theatre performed in galleries, empty storefronts, bars, and makeshift stages downtown, not to mention established but struggling performance spaces. This melee happened during August, when anyone who could afford to escape the suffocating heat of Manhattan could, leaving the rest of us to broil for our art.

The scale of the festival was daunting: two hundred or so shows produced by theatre kids from all over the world, sleeping on couches and eating knishes and doing their thing in one of dozens of venues, half of which were inadequate in unique and different ways. The shows ran the gamut, from intense, personal explorations of trauma to pop culture–drenched pageants engineered to be smash hits, each performed by a single actor from middle-of-nowhere Kansas or a tight-knit crew of hungry, howling theatre kids from Chicago or Philly or Richmond. Generally speaking, youth is wasted on the young, but it was not wasted at the Fringe. It was rocket fuel. The festival was a sophisticated operation, despite the chaos and low budget. The producers were interested in hits and more than a few, over the years, were produced, most notably the musical *Urinetown*, a crude but brilliant comedy about a dystopian future where private toilets are illegal that had an unlikely run on Broadway. But for the most part, the Fringe was small beans, which meant the politics were more bare-knuckle than you'd expect, poets and performance artists and directors stabbing each other in the back if it meant a better theater, maybe one with air conditioning or a more favorable time slot.

The Fringe taught me everything I ever needed to know about marketing, and those skills turned out to be helpful in my pursuit of a paycheck. I was under the impression that I—an artist—was above self-promotion, but I was not. The Fringe participants wanted an audience: everyone had paid an application fee but that was the least of the expenses, which included travel, food, and large, colorful papier-mâché hats.

If you were a nobody from out of town or a local with a play who couldn't afford an ad in one of the weeklies or proper street posters, you were left with one option: produce inexpensive fliers and postcards that you would scatter around the city like leaflets dropped from enemy planes during wartime.

My main takeaway from studying hundreds of postcards over the years is never to mention the word "theatre" when promoting theatre. No, the best theatre postcards I ever saw looked like they were invites to underground punk rock shows. That's Marketing 101: never sell the product. Sell a feeling instead.

The entire downtown theatre scene—especially the Fringe—was powered by two primary energies: One was a burning desire for success, to make a hit. To make it on Broadway or in Hollywood. The other energy was the drive to create uncompromising work, to create art that reflects something that's inside of you, to create something singular that rejects the idea that the only way to be successful is to make money. These two forces were in complete and total philosophical opposition.

There are other reasons to make theatre besides glory. The theatre has always provided reasons to drink, not that I ever needed an excuse. Lousy show? Drink! Triumphant performance? Drink! I'm broke, I'm depressed, I have to move back home? Drink! The Fringe also offered opportunities for the community to bond and connect and party, especially late at night. I spent many wee hours with downtown goons and pixies and other trouble-makers drinking bottles of the cheapest rotgut possible on empty, post-show stages.

During one of those late-night Fringe salons, we spun tales about how we escaped our miserable, boring, intolerant hometowns, and a few survivors of New York's lower depths would talk about the last ten years. These midnight gatherings ping-ponged between raucous demon party and the quiet intimacy of a lifeboat. There were confessions, and admissions. Fears and fantasies were shared. And gossip. Oh, yes, gossip. If there's one thing theatre kids love more than retelling their fabulous origin stories, it's being a bitch behind people's backs. Who's fucking who? How much did that show cost? Which director is a monster to their cast? Theatre kids also love retelling legends, and a legend is the truth wearing lipstick and a wig. Here's one legend I remember:

Joe Cino ran the fabled Caffe Cino in Greenwich Village, which opened in 1958, and Ellen Stewart ran La Mama Etc, the experimental theater in the East Village that launched the careers of Sam Shepard, Harvey Fierstein, and Bette Midler, to name a few. The doors to her theater opened in 1961.

Those two unlikely impresarios practically created Off-Off-Broadway, although betrothed hippie-anarchists Julian Beck and Judith Malina of the Living Theatre deserve credit as well—those two had been performing weird art pieces in lofts and storefronts for years—as does absurdist playwright Edward Albee, who supported Off-Off-Broadway even as his literary star rocketed skyward. I should also note that the gender-bending satirist Charles Ludlum and his campy Ridiculous Theatrical Company were significant contributors to this scene as well, lest Ludlam mock me in full-on drag from beyond the grave.

So, the legend. It went like this: Stewart held vigil over Cino as he died in the hospital. It was 1967 and he was thirty-five years old. He had been found in a pool of blood on the stage of the cafe one morning, having repeatedly stabbed himself in the stomach and arms with a knife. I forget who told me this story, but I know it was late at night during the Fringe, and I was most certainly drunk. I remember listening intently and questioning nothing. Stewart was there with him as the doctors and nurses at St. Vincent's changed his bandages and pumped him full of antibiotics, but he only lasted a few days.

Stewart was a fashion designer by trade but spent most of her time nurturing a community of near-feral theatre rebels. Her theater was constantly being shut down by cops in the early years. They also raided Cino because if there was one thing the city hated more than a black woman running a business, it was a gay man running a business.

Stewart was stylish and noble, a formidable artist. She had moved to New York in 1950. Her past was murky; she was born either in Chicago or in the middle of nowhere in Louisiana. Was she married? Divorced? Who knows? One day, she appeared in the East Village, like Athena springing forth from the head of Zeus.

Cino was a friendly, working-class bulldog from Buffalo who had wanted to become a dancer. He opened a coffeehouse because that was trendy in the early '60s, and then he discovered his true calling, which was running an orphanage for lovable freaks and giving playwrights like Lanford Wilson and María Irene Fornés a home. His small stage saw multiple performances a night: ambitious, bizarre, personal plays and musicals. Joe's Caffee Cino was where queer artists could be their true selves, and the first hit was a play about a drag queen.

The Caffee itself was snug, crammed with tables and chairs surrounding an 8×8 platform made out of milk cartons where dozens of shambolic productions were mounted, and in the back, a giant espresso machine would hiss. The walls were decorated with Christmas lights, adding to the space's warmth and sense of safety. When Caffee Cino was packed, audiences would sit on the cigarette machine.

Cino's establishment was a home for those running away from a world that would have preferred they lie about who they were inside, a world that defined love narrowly and cruelly. These small, muscular theaters were both magnets for the human beings America wanted to ignore.

Caffee Cino and La Mama were in conversation with each other both creatively and professionally. It was them against the snobs and the hoity-toities uptown. When Caffee Cino caught fire in '65, Stewart offered Cino's tight-knit group of actors and playwrights a home while he rebuilt.

Village Voice critic Jerry Tallmer was the first to use "Off-Off-Broadway" when describing the riot of rule-breaking theatre erupting in Greenwich Village featuring young new artists who weren't welcome on Broadway or Off-Broadway.

The term started as one critic's classification of a quasi-movement, but it instantly morphed into something more defiant and tongue-in-cheek. Off-Off-Broadway was the opposite of what the lame-os were politely applauding uptown. It was irreverent and impolite. It didn't take itself too seriously. "I'm doing a play. Where? Broadway—Off-Off-Broadway." That's one of my favorite jokes.

No one knew why Joe did what he did. Maybe he was distraught over the death of his boyfriend, John Torrey, a few months before. Maybe drugs? It didn't matter—he was loved and mourned. As Stewart and other loved ones crowded his hospital room, Cino's friends—his orphans, his community—got on their hands and knees and scrubbed the stage of Caffee Cino clean of gore.

* * *

I met Michael after seeing *Something Something Über Alles* at the Kraine. He knew David. Everyone knew David. We shook hands outside and talked about what we had seen, and how much we loved it. We were both gloriously shell-shocked. I agreed with everything he said. Wasn't Bani fabulous? Bold? Terrifying? Yes, yes, yes.

Michael was a real-life bohemian. That was my first impression. I could tell from the moment I met him that he had big plans. Big art plans. Michael was skinny but confident and graceful. A weathered leather mariner's cap sat atop his curly locks, which made him look like an easygoing Bolshevik. He smiled at me, like he just heard a silly joke, and I smiled back.

Part of my plan was to meet strange and extraordinary people like me, and Michael was one of those people, even though he was a nice Jewish boy from the Maryland suburbs with a head full of dreams. But if he had told me he was from Europe, from one of the great cafe cities like Vienna or Prague or Paris, the old world's intellectual capitals, I would have believed him.

He would be mortified to be described as a bohemian. I don't think Michael saw himself as a free spirit. He was an artist who worked at a law firm, a job that he never complained about. We drank black coffee like a pair of civilized intellectuals the first time we hung out just the two of us. We met at the Astor Place Starbucks, which had opened in 1995, an omen of the gentrification to come, but back then, the managers were putting blacklights in the restrooms so the East Village junkies couldn't find their veins.

Michael wasn't a drinker, which I thought was so sophisticated. He wasn't a teetotaler either, but he was content not hanging out at a bar. So we hunched over our overpriced dark roasts and blah-blah-blahed with the enthusiasm of teen girls talking about hunks.

He was full of opinions—not sneering criticisms, the mother tongue of posers and dilettantes, but bright, shiny statements of belief. He talked about the theatre and movies and music that moved him, he just effortlessly sang love songs about the stuff that hoisted his heart skyward, and then he'd ask me questions and listened to my answers and I learned a valuable lesson that night, and it was that most people don't have original opinions. Most people parrot what they read or hear and then regurgitate it with confidence, plagiarizing and bluffing but rarely sharing what they really think and feel—having thoughts takes work. And part of that work is knowing how to listen too.

Michael was brave, in a way, and I clocked that from day one: he was willing to be who he was, come hell or high water, while I prayed, every night, to be anyone but me, or at least, to be a better, more intelligent, more handsome, more compassionate me.

He was one of the first people to ask me questions about my plays and my plans, to take me seriously, and I did my best to return the favor. He gave his respect so easily and I wanted to earn it. He once asked me about my favorite Stephen Sondheim musicals, and the only one I knew was *Into the Woods*, his deconstruction of popular fairy tales with lyrics by James Lapine.

The original Broadway production starring Bernadette Peters as a cackling witch was filmed for PBS in 1991, and my mom taped it on the VCR. I watched it while sick one afternoon, and then I rewound it and watched it again.

Into the Woods is a musical about death, family, and fidelity, but it's also about honesty and how parents should be careful what they tell their children. The songs were catchy, but underneath the playful melodies and the many jokes was a voice telling me things are not what they seem. I didn't love the musical as much as *Les Misérables*, but I realized that musicals could be more than just singing and dancing.

But my answer to his question couldn't be *Into the Woods*. That choice seemed too obvious; it was one of Sondheim's most famous works. And Michael had asked me my favorite musicals, plural. So I said, "Who can choose?"

A few months later, Michael had cast me in his adaptation of Dostoyevsky's novella *Notes from the Underground*, which starred his theatrical collaborator Robert as the infamous narrator, a drunken nineteenth-century Moscovite pencil-pusher who cannot connect with other human beings.

You wouldn't think they were members of l'avant-garde by looking at them: Robert was a bankruptcy lawyer during the day and an actor at night.

He had left his comfortable life in Houston to move to New York. He was cordial and intense and his very slight Texas twang reminded me of my kin. He had gone to all the right schools and had a promising career and yet he still wanted nothing more than to work with Michael, a nice guy with a day job who read difficult books by Russians and looked up to the work of wildman directors like Grotowski and Foreman.

Dostoevsky's slim but influential 1864 masterpiece is one long locomotive of a monologue spewed by this disgruntled Russian man who wallows in regret and self-loathing, reliving his professional and romantic failures in a spiral of derangement. The character heralds the arrival of a new kind of modern man, the lone wolf, the alienated nobody, a lost and angry boy. Robert's performance was coiled, like a noose, and he intuitively understood that sometimes rage is fear on a mission. His "underground man" was a rat trapped in an infinite loop of grief—grief over his entire wasted life. It was a tour de force and I had never observed a tour de force up close and personal: Robert was prepared and focused, friendly and collaborative. And when the show started, he was a different person: an animal, hiding in the dark, hissing at ghosts.

I was one of four chorus members who would wear contemporary clothes and blend in with an audience that Michael would lead down the treacherous steps of the sidewalk cellar of an East Village art gallery. The audience—all eight of them—would crowd into this basement and sit uncomfortably on stacks of books as Robert lit actual oil-filled lamps with matches and ranted, until the chorus revealed itself as four voices representing the underground man's disintegrating mental health. This was not a show for anyone claustrophobic or afraid of dying in a basement fire.

It was a successful run and it achieved all of Michael's goals, which mostly consisted of disorienting paying customers. Michael had a talent for literary interpretation and in another dimension, he'd be an impressive scholar.

Instead, he turned into a sort of benevolent literary vandal. He understood that Dostoyevsky's "underground man" was funny not because he's bitter and lonely, but because he lacks any self-awareness. He's a melodramatic clown feeling sorry for himself, and Robert's performance, guided by Michael's direction, emphasized this, and they turned a character worshipped by literary bros into a pitiful buffoon.

I found the show exciting and I did an excellent job as one of the ghosts haunting Robert's character, and I attribute that to not having many lines. I was able to memorize them all, almost perfectly. I had not felt such a current before as an actor, and it only served to validate my decision to embrace the obscurity and destitution and freedom that only Off-Off-Broadway could offer.

For a brief moment, I entertained a new dream: posthumous icon.

The gravity of Michael's show attracted other wannabe theatre renegades, feral and overeducated (but not at any of the art schools that mattered). I don't know exactly what a "theatre renegade" is, but I remember wanting to be one, an underappreciated genius who spoke up for the common man. I read Genet and Sartre and Ionesco. I studied the social clichés. I drank red wine, which is one of the slowest and most inefficient ways for one to get hammered, but I sipped discount Merlots for the aesthetic. I learned, slowly, to despise wine. I hated how it stained the teeth too. I wrote poems on cocktail napkins and I railed against the bourgeoisie even though I was pretty sure I was a member of the bourgeoisie.

I wanted a life of truth and beauty and pleasure, although the whole dying penniless thing did strike me as, possibly, unnecessary, but I ignored that part. I was young! And I was not alone with this ridiculous fantasy. I was not the only member of the "They'll Appreciate Me When I'm Dead" club.

For about a month or two, after *Notes from Underground* closed, a group of us gathered at Charas Community Center on 9th Street near Avenue C, a huge old public school that had been turned into a community center and offered inexpensive rehearsal space. Two years later, it would be sold off to a developer by Mayor Giuliani, the Republican and former federal prosecutor whose combative mayoral administration was mostly known for police violence until 9/11 turned him into a national hero. If that horror had not happened, he would have been quickly forgotten, his only legacy his attempts to dismantle neighborhoods by selling off buildings to cronies that actual families and nonprofit organizations used.

The group—which I cheekily nicknamed The Legion of Doom—was made up of a rotating cast of grown adults who spent their days fermenting in offices uptown. We were all drones in one way or another, except Robert, who contributed to society as an attorney. I think, ultimately, that was his greatest role, his life's work: acting like a successful lawyer.

I was fortunate to be working as an editorial lackey and my managers either were oblivious or turned a blind eye to the many ways I would rip off my employer: I used resources I shouldn't have all the time, either printing dozens of copies of scripts I'd written on company paper during company time or sneaking actors into the office after hours to use meeting rooms as rehearsal spaces. I used to call this the "art tax," and I thought corporate America could afford it.

Our jobs were a means to an end; they were not our identity. They were just parts we'd play. I'd get up in the morning and take the train to 57th Street and check facts and take notes during editorial meetings and once the clock read five, I'd hurtle on a southbound train to get to where the fun was, and the drugs, and the emotionally volatile refugees from regular America.

I stole the name of the group from a Sunday morning cartoon superhero series called *Super Friends*. The Legion of Doom was a group of supervillains dedicated to fighting the Justice League, and its members included classic baddies like Superman's nemesis Lex Luthor and The Riddler, one of two

Batman villains on the bench. The group wasn't fond of "Legion of Doom." But it stuck because no one else came up with an alternative. I thought it was funny, but in retrospect, perhaps it was too frivolous. We were supposed to be serious artists. At least, I think that was the plan? My favorite member of the animated Legion of Doom was Gorilla Grodd, a super-intelligent, telepathic ape.

The group's purpose was to share and critique new work that could be developed into a full-fledged production paid for by credit card that would run for a few weekends for tens of people. We also spent time gossiping about other obscure, small-time downtown theatre companies and the nobodies who ran them, and we kibbitzed as if these were the most important people in the world. We'd performatively sneered at Broadway, too, which we all agreed was corporate swill that was rotting the American soul, especially *Rent*, the musical that made squatting sexy.

There are two primary types of theatre kids in the world: those who adore the musical *Rent* and those who hate it, and I hated it. I thought it was a touchy-feely, soft-boiled pop opera tragedy about, well, theatre kids slumming it in New York City. And for a show about heroin and AIDS and economic struggle, it was squeaky-clean and confident, like The Gap.

It was hugely popular then, partly due to the tragic death of its young creator, Jonathan Larson, on the night of *Rent*'s Off-Broadway premiere. His passing was a shock and a loss. But I knew so many people my age who saw themselves in the chic bohemians and sassy slackers in *Rent* and I judged each of them, harshly. There were years I couldn't attend a party without someone telling me the damn musical was based on Puccini's 1896 opera *La Bohème*. I couldn't escape it.

The Legion of Doom understood, though.

This little gang lasted for a few months, and it was an exciting and creative time. During those weeks, we'd show up after our day gigs with monologues written during lunch hours and excerpts from obscure classics like Georg Büchner's unfinished, expressionistic, proto-Brechtian play *Woyzeck*, which was mostly unknown to civilians (and me). I brought sketches I had written inspired by television and my favorite playwright at the time, David Mamet, America's macho dramatist extraordinaire, whose plays were all about fast-talking dirtbags. I was enamored of Mamet's rat-a-tat machine gun–style dialogue, peppered with obscenities and interruptions. I discovered his most famous play, *Glengarry Glen Ross*, in high school and was shocked that a play could have the F-word and C-word in it, even though the play itself is a bore, a half-dozen Willy Lomans verbally abusing each other. Mamet is the worst kind of theatre kid, and that's a theatre kid who hates theatre kids, and maybe that's why he tried so hard over so many years to drench his plays in testosterone. Mamet's theatre is full of unsmiling, cheerless heterosexual men busting each other's balls forever.

One member of the Legion, Susanna, brought pieces of an unfinished one-person play about the chaos we all feared was lurking at the end of the millennium, and Hope and Jeff, a pair of collaborators who were also dating, offered up sneak peeks of their unpredictable, cartoon-inspired aesthetic. Hope and Jeff also had the distinction of being the last of Bani's students at Bard, a renowned upstate college for flower children and ne'er-do-wells. He had been fired for asking a student provocative and embarrassing questions about her sex life during class.

Bani could be rude, and worse, he could be cruel, and his passion for life and art was only equaled by a quiet rage, an anger at the world, at the scolds and prudes and young Americans who have so much and don't even know it.

Every so often, he would make an appearance, and we would swoon when he entered one of the large rooms we'd rent, some of which were classrooms with chalkboards. We'd either bore him with our performances or excite him, and he'd immediately let us know which. Bani was a theatre kid from birth, it was obvious. Some of us are called, but some are born with a talent for making grand entrances and filling rooms with our voice and light.

Bani moved slowly, and gracefully, like the Pope. A flamboyant Pope. But he was also spring-loaded. Powerful. The man could pounce.

He was always smoking and purring and pointing. Bani was in his fifties, and he was hustling as much as any of us. He would teach the odd class here or there, and I'd attend when I could afford his fee, which he would occasionally waive. I wasn't one of his favorites but we clicked. Whenever he'd see me, he'd bellow, "DEVOOOOOOOORE," and his eyes would twinkle, and he'd hug me, tightly. Bani and I had so many things in common, like drinking. The Legion hung on his every word, even the obscene ones or the ones that made little sense.

He relished questioning your artistic choices, especially in a class setting while you were making those choices. Bani played the jester, too—an affable, learned goofball and destroyer—and he wanted his young charges to mock orthodoxy and jeer at sacred cows.

He once shocked me by casually dismissing Shakespeare's tragedies as "all crucifixion, no resurrection." He never said it directly, but I got the sense he felt the same way about the West. Bani loved Jesus. Jesus was a good, Middle Eastern boy who preached a message of radical love that the savages didn't want to hear.

Bani despised moralizers and elitists. He had nothing kind to say about the right-wing religious fanatics that ruined his country, but I never got the sense that he was comfortable around pious liberals and their polite and judgmental politics.

After our workshops, we'd frequently pick one of a half-dozen Indian restaurants on 6th Street where you could feast for very little money while a performer played traditional Indian music on a sitar. These were all bring-your-own booze establishments, so we would sneak in plastic bottles of hobo vodka and pour them into mango lassis, and we'd order piles of naan and split plates of saag paneer and chicken vindaloo and talk about art and our plans for the future, the plays we wanted to write or direct, making sure to ask Bani what he thought of this or that, and if he was in good spirits or not quite wasted, he'd hold court and lecture us about the exquisiteness of Polish theatre director Jerzy Grotowski.

Bani had been raised Assyrian-Presbyterian in Tehran, and had studied theology and art, and he was moved by the French dramatist Antonin Artaud, whose "theatre of cruelty" sought to shock modern audiences out of their complacency. His exile was painful, which was clear, and unlike me, he had a reason to drink and that's why, later, at any number of dark East Village bars, when we were all good and fucked up, I'd forgive him his wandering hands and probing fingers and occasional hot breath in my ear.

But those were wonderful dinners. We took our time and got drunk and told each other our secrets, and the next morning we'd forget them. Not all of them, though. I remember a few. For instance, Michael was once cast as Jean Valjean in a summer theatre camp production of *Les Misérables* at the age of fifteen.

* * *

When a playwright or actor asks "What did you think?" after a theatre performance, it is customary to respond as cheerfully and vaguely as possible.

No one who asks "What did you think?" wants an honest answer. But no one wants to be deceived, either. So tread delicately. First, be affirming. "It was wonderful" suffices. You can follow up with any of these: "What a unique production." "I thought it was complex." Or, "What did *you* think?"

If the show is irredeemably awful, you can always compliment the costumes, and David couldn't even compliment the costumes. I had asked him to come to the very sloppy rehearsal of a play I had written, a real production.

Afterward, over bottom-shelf scotches, he looked at me solemnly and said, "Don't let the press see it."

"The press? Like the *New York Times*?" Luckily for me, the *New York Times* had never responded to multiple desperate emails from me inviting them to a dilapidated downtown theater that smelled like mold.

When I asked him pointedly what he thought of the play, he winced, and I groaned. He didn't say "You'll never work in this town again," but that's what I heard. I trusted David to tell me the truth. I didn't expect him actually to tell me the truth, though. I downed my drink and then another and thought about my career or lack thereof.

David didn't have to mention the director. He knew I knew. The director was a quiet and soft-spoken German man about my age with ambitions of his own and when my back was turned, he rearranged my words, my precious words, and turned my comedy sketches into surrealist theatrical vignettes, expressionistic and inscrutable.

The German, as I called him, had come to New York to explore and experiment and make art. For a few weeks, we'd have long, emotional discussions about the meaning of theatre, but ultimately, I just wanted to be popular. He wouldn't accept that. The German tried to save me from myself and failed.

The cast was mostly drawn from bright-eyed kids right off the bus from nowhere and New Jersey. They were all members of the theater's repertory company, which required every actor to audition and to work around the venue for free to get on stage. A few lived upstairs from the theater and rented small, inexpensive rooms and crawlspaces. I called them the People Under the Stairs.

The play was bad, and it would never improve. But I tried. The next day, I insisted on an emergency meeting with Edith, the woman producing my play. We sat on the lumpy couch in the musty lobby of her Off-Off-Broadway theater right before the box office opened.

She was eighty-two at the time. I was twenty-four.

I told her what David had said, and she smiled serenely. Shrugged. Usually, she answered my questions with stories. But not this time, which frustrated me. I think of her often. More than I ever thought I would. She died at 103 in the fall of 2020 when everyone was still terrified of the plague and hiding inside. The theaters were closed.

But this time she just listened to me as I melted down. I wanted to know why . . . why my play wasn't sold out. I wanted to know why the *New York Times* had not sent a critic. I wanted to know what I was doing with my life.

Was I high when I asked these questions? Yes. Was I drunk? Also, yes. A little.

I was a serious playwright with a goatee (the goatee was back) and a notebook full of titles to plays that would never be written to prove it. I had managed to write a few messy short plays during my lunch breaks as an assistant editor at a trade magazine. One of the plays was a rude little sex comedy titled *JFK vs. the UFOs*. In that play, a lascivious, amphetamine-fueled Jack Kennedy tortures an extraterrestrial wiseass. Another was a dark story about a temp working for a company trying to secretly kill its employees with free poisoned coffee and exploding office equipment.

And then there was the current play, *The Meatgrinder Waltz*, which was my masterpiece. "This is my ticket," I'd thought, "to fame and fortune." I had decided to sell out, and why not? America is a pirate nation that only prizes profit and plunder.

My love affair with self-produced plays that put me into credit card debt had begun to cool by the last year of the twentieth century. I wasn't alone, either. My equally broke and frustrated contemporaries started referring to their work as "indie," like the popular '90s movie movement. It was still Off-Off-Broadway, unfairly or not.

So, I had decided to write a play that would be popular. Forget plays about the human condition or socialism or nightmare sex comedies. I was going to write a play that would spark a revolution. Specifically: a revolution of my fortunes.

I remember reading the word "feted" in a profile in *New York Magazine* or *Vanity Fair* of some young vicious member of the literati and thinking, "I want to be feted." At the time I read the article, the precise definition of "feted" eluded me, but I knew I wanted it, whatever it was, and I hoped it had something to do with money and fame.

Then something unexpected happened: I had met Edith, and she had agreed to produce *The Meatgrinder Waltz* in her small Off-Off-Broadway theater on 13th Street near Union Square. Actual real-life actors would be speaking my precious words in New York City? I changed my mind slightly. You know, maybe Off-Off-Broadway wasn't so bad?

The cramped Thirteenth Street Repertory Theatre was in the basement of a crumbling rowhouse built in the 1840s. According to myth, it had once been a stop on the Underground Railroad. There were sixty-five seats in the theater, and each one was broken in a different subtle way from the others, so it didn't really matter where you sat because you would never be comfortable. The theater's main claim to fame was that it was home to the longest-running play in Off-Off-Broadway history, Israel Horowitz's absurdist drama *Line*. It's about five people waiting in line for a nameless event. It had been running for almost twenty-five years when I first met Edith.

Edith had moved from Idaho to Greenwich Village in the early 1970s to make art and be part of the legendary Off-Off-Broadway scene. And Edith loved Off-Off-Broadway. The rawness of it, the promise. The "Hey, let's put on a show!" vibe. She lived on the third floor and would slowly descend downstairs every morning to the theater. She once offhandedly mentioned the time that the great Southern-fried playwright Tennessee Williams had stumbled into her theater and proceeded to pass out drunk during a performance.

A friend of Yvonne had introduced me to Edith, and over the course of a few weeks, I had convinced (sweet-talked, groveled, beseeched) her to put on a collection of my short plays. She called them sketches, but the difference between sketches and my short plays was simple: A sketch is funny. My short plays were funny but also scathing indictments of society.

Or that was what I told myself late at night. I suspected the truth, of course. They were sketches, amusing and derivative, obviously inspired by television shows like *Saturday Night Live* and *The Kids in the Hall.*

I was not the first young straight white man with an ego like a dandelion puff who thought he was the second coming of Samuel Beckett that she had dealt with over the decades. The more imperial I became, the more beatific her responses.

Edith was the first adult who wasn't a family member or teacher to take me remotely seriously. She wasn't paying me, but I chose to believe we mutually exploited each other. She provided me with a stage, actors, and lights, and I supplied my genius. This arrangement meant she'd give me rehearsal and script notes I hated and then chuckle when I protested.

The production was troubled from the start. Doomed. The German was fired a few weeks into the run, and the cast revolted. The show was plodding— a snooze performed by dabblers, and my precious words didn't help. No one came to see it. I went almost every night and squirmed. Sometimes, it was just me and one of Edith's renters. I got a bad review on a blog that no one read. I left a nasty comment.

A few weeks later, another young, professional director named RJ would be hired to save the show, and while he was talented, he wasn't a miracle worker. I use the words "fired" and "hired" because they make the most sense, but these were not jobs. No one was being paid. The drama of it all stressed me out to the point that I started eating antacids like they were Halloween candy.

Edith took everything in stride. She had seen and heard it all before. Nothing is more infuriating than someone who refuses to lose their mind with you. Edith loved the theatre enough to put up with all the theatre kids. I never saw her again after the show closed.

The Meatgrinder Waltz opened April 2. The title was changed halfway through the run to *Nuts and Bolts* in an attempt to erase the German's crimes against art, a pivot that RJ and I agreed was for the best. It closed December 1, and by the next day, I decided to retire from Off-Off-Broadway. Yet, somehow, Off-Off-Broadway soldiered on.

II
THE MISERABLE

Five years later.

I was almost thirty years old during the winter of 2004, the same age as Hamlet, and like Shakespeare's moody prince, I didn't know whether to be or not to be. Is that sentiment melodramatic? Yes. It is. Quite. But I felt I had a few things in common with the famous Dane: I enjoyed brooding and talking to myself. And we both had dead dads.

I was fond of stumbling home inebriated, stripping naked, and then addressing the universe—mostly protests and criticisms and thoughts on the misery that is existence—and here's where my story diverges from Hamlet's: I was never visited by any ghost. My old man did not reach out to me from the beyond. Also, I was not as cynical as Hamlet. I was, simply, angry. How dare he die? I was angry at myself too. There had been times I could have visited him, but I chose to pickle myself instead. I was also angry at Jesus H. Christ, who my dad had assured me was watching over us .

Maybe he was. Maybe he was eating popcorn too. The last time I ever prayed was one night in 2002 when I begged the Son of Man to spare my dad's life. I even got on my knees, the way I was taught to pray at night, before bedtime. The response was "No." He didn't speak to me. I didn't hear his voice. The cancer just did its thing.

There is nothing anyone can say after you lose someone you love, and that never stops people from trying. It's just human nature. I found no comfort in anyone's words or hugs or promises that it would get better, which was something I was not inclined to believe at the time. The verdict is still out.

Nothing made me squirm more than being told, "Time heals all wounds." I knew that bit of dusty wisdom was meant to comfort me, but I'd always mumble something like "time doesn't heal pulmonary carcinoma" under my breath in response.

In the weeks after my dad's death, I had begun to push family away slowly—aunts and uncles and cousins at first—but not before I had been told about the five stages of grief that would deliver me from my pain. Magic words. These five stages would also hurry up the mourning process—the sobbing, and moping—which is pretty depressing to watch.

The five stages are denial, anger, bargaining, depression, and acceptance. The idea is the grieving process is linear, and once you experience each stage, you move on from your sorrow and return to the land of the living, where everyone pretends like they're never going to die. I discovered that the stages don't always happen one after the other. Sometimes, you get stuck in one stage. Sometimes, the five stages of grief happen all at once.

And then there's the sixth stage of grief, which is oblivion. Nothingness. A dimension where I didn't exist, where I was freed from the agony of loving and being loved. This is the stage no one brings up. The stage you have to find on your own. The sixth stage of grief was the desire to occupy a new reality different from my current one, a place where my father was never born and neither was I, a place where neither joy nor sorrow could reach me, a place detached from the now.

I accepted that my dad had died. I just didn't want to carry that pain, and I didn't want to put it down, either. I didn't want his memory. I wanted to forget. I wanted to float, to barely even exist, like a whisper or an April snowflake. So I drank. It was easy to do, a simple, joyless lunge of despair. The liquor was *waiting* for me there, in that place where I was no one's son or brother or friend—that place at the bottom of a great, cold darkness, just me and a bottle.

What I know now—what I didn't know then—was that I would have found that great cold darkness, and the bottle, even if he had lived, or had never even gotten sick in the first place. I know I had a good reason to anesthetize myself. But I was born to drink. It is who I am and I had little choice in the matter.

Two years later and I still couldn't accept what had happened; I couldn't wrap my heart around the sudden violence of it. I had known he was dying, but then it happened, and the world was cleaved into two: there was the world as it was, with my family and friends and all my responsibilities living there, and then there was my fourth-floor walk-up in Queens, where I could pass out in the bathtub if I wanted. To be or not to be? Not to be, *por favor*.

I had a nightmare that still haunts me all these years later: I dreamt of his lung, the one that was removed, a pinkish-gray sack covered in tumors the color of rot, and I dreamed that it was sitting in some pan in the back of some medical refrigerator, and that it was still pulsing and breathing and living, and that I had to find his organ and hold the wiggling wet mass in my arms.

That nightmare was vivid and unique because my nights had been dreamless that winter. I'd black out and bliss would follow. The alcohol helped put me to sleep, and, ironically, it helped wake me up. My days were long and full of sitting on the subway and in front of a computer, and at a bar. I had other distractions in my life that didn't come in a shot glass or hoovered up through a tightly rolled dollar bill. I read comic books. I spent hours walking up and down the aisles of Blockbuster Video where'd I rent unloved sequels to some of my favorite cinematic classics: *Gremlins 2, Robocop 2, Predator 2.*

I also had my career, or what passed as a career.

The life of a serious playwright is not easy, especially if you don't have connections, or a trust fund, or talent. This is why I started writing for the internet around 2000 or so, a year that still sounds futuristic, as if it hasn't happened yet.

In the rigid hierarchy of New York's literary and publishing scenes at the time, writing for a blog or website was a rung below that of a subway ad copywriter, even though that paid well. When I took my first dot-com gig in 2000, an older editor told me it would ruin my career.

He might have been right? In the long run?

But four years later, in 2004, I was working for the cable TV channel Comedy Central's website, where I wrote variations on promo copy that read like this: "It's like the news, only funny! Tune in to *The Daily Show* with Jon Stewart, 11 EST/10 CST, only on Comedy Central."

I got the job because Comedy Central had bought my previous employer for pennies on the dollar during the dot-com bust. My former employer had been a site called Jokes.com. For years, I edited tens of thousands of corny/dirty/profoundly unfunny zingers, knee-slappers, and other assorted gags, all submitted by drooling teenage boys and their dads.

I reinterviewed for my old job and was rehired with a few new responsibilities. This new position was referred to as "permalance," which meant it had all the responsibility of a job without any benefits, including, most notably, health insurance. I once paid a doctor out-of-pocket because I had a chest cold and needed antibiotics. He wrote me a prescription and told me to cut back on the cigarettes and booze. I acted shocked that he would imply I was smoking and drinking too much, but we both knew that was bullshit. He could tell I was brining myself nightly. I was bloated and pasty, and if he had taken a blood sample, the results would have come back with a celery stalk.

The Comedy Central job also didn't pay much, even though I sometimes saw celebrities walk around. I urinated next to the comedian Dave Chappelle occasionally, which was cool. We never made eye contact, but, hey, show business.

* * *

I don't remember exactly when I bought my first cell phone, but it was sometime during the ten months separating 9/11 and my father's death from cancer in July of 2002. I remember the model: a classic silver Motorola flip-phone that looked like a large silver beetle when closed.

I had spent the last few years of the previous century committed to using payphones to check my voicemail but surrendered after the chaos of the terrorist attacks, even though cell service was pretty much useless for hours after the towers fell. I managed to get through to my dad on an office landline later that day, and he sounded out of breath, gasping for air. I thought it was the end of the world, and he fought back tears as he told me to get home to Queens as soon as I could, to get out of Manhattan as quickly as possible.

But I realized I had to get a cell phone after reading the stories of people trapped on the hijacked planes calling their families from the air and leaving final, panicked messages of love.

One day I was blissfully unavailable to anyone who wanted to get in touch with me and the next I was a modern man on the go, gabbing away while walking down the middle of the street. I held on to that phone for years, until it was hopelessly obsolete, for sentimental reasons. I talked to my old man for the last time using that Motorola.

The phone buzzed on the bar as I waited for Michael. It was mid-January. 2004 was still young. I hated the sound of the buzzing. It could have been my mom, my sister, or a bill collector. I didn't pick up. I didn't want to talk to any of them. I didn't even look at who was calling. I just shut the thing off and ordered another bourbon and then another.

I had called Michael a few days before and left a message on his voicemail. I had dialed up other friends, too, but none of them returned my calls. Only Michael did. I had rehearsed a little voicemail speech that I hoped sounded casual, not desperate or scared. I felt like an alien trying to sound human but not too human. The message was short and sweet, basically "Hi. How are you? I am not doing well. Bye!"

It had been a while since I'd seen him. Months? Years? A century or two? I vaguely remembered bumping into him at some party in the East Village, a crowded, smoky little get-together, fueled by brandy and clove cigarettes and hosted by a sculptor/office manager whose so loved ornate throw pillows she filled her railroad apartment with them. I did not like brandy nor cloves, so I'd mouthed "goodbye" to Michael as he was arriving.

One of the last times we had spent significant time together was a few months after the 9/11 attacks when we went to a screening of Stanley Kubrick's 1968 sci-fi classic *2001: A Space Odyssey*, a movie I had never really seen until Michael invited me to behold it in majestic 70mm. I related to the monkeys, oblivious to God and history. After the movie, we talked about sandwiches on the moon and murderous computers.

He had called me, a couple of times, after my dad's death, but the conversations were brief. There's nothing to say: "Sorry for your loss" and then breathing. Awkward, comforting breathing. He had also left voicemails that I had ignored.

Michael agreed to meet me at a cavernous fake Irish pub in midtown Manhattan, which was a few blocks away from where I worked. It was friendly to tourists and office dwellers. I would frequently crash-land there the minute work was over to toss back a few before jumping on a train uptown and then into Queens, where I would then head to a bar close to my apartment.

I hadn't been venturing south of 14th Street for a while. The city was still divided into uptown and downtown, with midtown serving as a crowded purgatory of office buildings. Uptown was for clean-cut corporate androids who ate salads for lunch, and downtown was for tattooed hooligans with one or two college degrees.

Brooklyn was another city entirely. Queens? Another country. And the Bronx? A rumor.

The pub smelled fresh and clean—a mix of lemon cleaning solution and hoppy beers—due to the total ban on indoor smoking that New York City had enacted ten months prior. It was a civilizing law that most people supported—it turns out drinking in a filthy ashtray was not popular, except for those of us wallowing in the stink.

I spent the last night before the ban went into effect bravely declaring I would NEVER smoke outside, and I was smoking outside when I saw Michael walking up. He was on time. As he approached I opened the door to the pub, bowed respectfully, and said, "You first."

Michael was tired-looking but in good spirits. He wore his trademark leather hat, the one that made him look like an underachieving nineteenth-century anarchist. I was surprised at how happy I was to see Michael because his friendliness always put me off. But he smiled when he saw me, and I felt a sense of safety, albeit briefly.

The conversation was initially strained, dueling "How are you?"s. I was well, and so was he. Then a pause. He was cheerful with the bartender and ordered a beer that he would nurse for our entire time together. We were both single. His family was happy and healthy, and I hadn't spoken to my family in months. I hadn't even gone home for Christmas.

We talked about what everyone was talking about, which was the wars in the Middle East.

There were two dominant opinions at that time, the first being what the majority thought of President Bush's invasions of Afghanistan and Iraq: Fuck 'em up. The country wanted revenge. America had given itself permission to lash out, to hunt and torture and kill the people responsible for all those horrible deaths downtown and at the Pentagon. And if the people we were bombing and killed weren't directly responsible? So be it. U.S.A.! U.S.A.!

The minority shared the other opinion: This is crazy. There were theatre companies making protest art, but most people didn't care about protesting or the anti-war movement, especially the media. By 2004, however, hundreds were being killed by suicide bombers in occupied Baghdad and smaller cities like Erbil and Hillah. The dead also included American troops, but mostly the victims were Iraqi civilians and soldiers. That violence began to put a damper on the bloodlust. The warmongers weren't quite as merry as they were in 2003.

So Michael and I chatted about politics and the hopelessness of it all. I tried to lighten up the conversation but failed because I brought up Spalding Gray, the acclaimed downtown monologist and actor who had killed himself a few days earlier by jumping off the Staten Island Ferry. Gray had worked closely with Michael's teacher at NYU, the director Richard Schechner, who founded the influential experimental theatre company The Performance Group in 1967. Schechner was a theatrical innovator who coined the term "environmental theatre," merging ritual and drama to create intense, emotional, and intimate works, sometimes in non-traditional spaces.

A few years after the launch of The Performance Group, Gray and his spouse, director Elizabeth LeCompte, would form the Wooster Group and create autographical theatrical pieces based on Gray's life. The two theatre companies shared space until the '80s. Under the artistic direction of LeCompte, The Wooster Group became synonymous with edgy spectacles that would confound and terrify tourists and Broadway babies.

Michael had studied with Schechner at NYU in the '90s, and the director significantly influenced him. He wanted to create plays that swallowed the audience like a sea monster and transported them to different times and places, and he wanted to do that work with a group of like-minded artists, a tight-knit collective pushing each other to be better.

I think I made a *My Dinner with Andre* joke. Have you seen *My Dinner with Andre*? It was a hit arthouse movie from 1981 starring playwright and actor Wallace Shawn and theatre director André Gregory sitting down for a meal, two old friends who haven't seen each other in a while. It was a cult classic, quiet, cerebral, wry. It was the exact opposite of a superficial Hollywood blockbuster, just a pair of dudes eating and talking about life and art. Shawn is a grumpy cynic, and Gregory is a gentle explorer, hungry for connection. He's been on a great creative, exotic adventure overseas, where he met monks, actors, and the mystical, mysterious Jerzy Grotowski. If I made a joke, the punchline probably went like this: "I'm no Wallace Shawn and you're no André Gregory."

The conversation slowed until a silence hung between us like a birthday balloon losing its helium. He took a sip of his beer; I tossed back my drink. Then Michael leaned in and said, "How are you?"

By this point, I was good and tanked, so I told him. I opened my heart. I suddenly became a living, breathing, alcohol-powered machine that extruded long thick, wet ropes of anxiety and grief. How am I? Michael? Well, I was sad. Depressed. Lonely. I whined like a young Uncle Vanya.

I hadn't gone home for Christmas because the house was small and dark, and it reminded me of him, sitting in a recliner, playing video games, dying, and I spent New Year's Eve at my local, avoiding eye contact. How am I? Well, Michael, I was drinking too much. Chain-smoking. When I had pills, I ate them. Coke, weed, whatever. I wasn't writing plays. I was writing promotional copy for a cable television channel. I had sold out, but I was also broke. Then I told him that I had been having an affair with my coworker, a married woman named Julie who I thought I was in love with, and that her husband had found out and threatened to cut off my fingers. My fingers! I was so freaked out that I had applied for a job at a trashy men's magazine to get away from her. How am I? I'm pretty fucked up. Michael didn't have a response to any of what I shared, so I watched him watch me order yet another bourbon, and then I asked him how the theater was going—The Brick.

In 2002, Michael and Robert had rented and refurbished a brick-lined auto body shop–slash–yoga studio deep in Williamsburg, Brooklyn, and turned it into a nonprofit performance space complete with a lighting grid and risers and a new, sprung dance floor built by Michael's younger brother Darren, a carpenter and philosophy student.

If you want to lose large sums of money quickly and efficiently, it would be hard to beat opening a theater. Investing in a movie is risky, but there's also the chance that the movie will be a huge hit and make tons of money. There is no chance of that happening if you're a theater, especially one that wants to support emerging artists, which is the term of art for thespians and dramatists who are under the age of fifty and unemployed. If you're older and unemployed, you're a veteran.

New York City is a theater graveyard; every inch of this city's real estate has, at one time, been performed upon or considered by some self-appointed theatrical visionary as an ideal spot to stage a play, protest, or both. This is an enduring tale that ends poorly most of the time.

Did Michael and Robert know this before throwing their savings and paychecks down a bottomless hole? They're smart guys, but love makes people do crazy things.

They called their theater The Brick because that was what the walls were made of, and their goal was to produce the kind of experimental work that once flourished in Manhattan. Michael and Robert wanted a space to dream and play and create. They were an odd couple, of course, a courtly Texan and a soft-spoken Jewish boy, but they were also a pair of educated poindexters who shared an almost naive faith in the destructive and purifying power of the theatre. To them, theatre—live, hot-blooded theatre—was Important with a capital "I."

So they crossed the East River to industrial Brooklyn like all the other clowns who just wanted to make their dumb art and be left the hell alone.

You wouldn't think it by looking at them, but Robert and Michael, two normal men, had dedicated their lives to the revolution.

Michael tried to talk to me a bit about the ins and outs of managing a 501(c)(3) organization, but the whole idea of nonprofits perplexed me, like internships and taxes. The existence of nonprofit theaters that kept the lights on thanks to donations and grants was like science fiction. I didn't even know what a grant was. And despite all of this, The Brick still needed to get butts in seats to stay solvent. That's the contradictory madness at the heart of most nonprofits—the funding isn't always enough to keep the lights on. Theatres need audiences; they need hits.

The first few months of running The Brick had been a domestic comedy of errors. The space was a fixer-upper, with an emphasis on "fix." It was drafty in the winter and unbearable in the summer. It could seat around sixty comfortably, or more if people sat on the floor. The toilet was stuffed in the corner and above was a tech booth built for a hobbit and the only way into it was up a creaky, perilous ladder. Sometimes, Michael would spend hours sitting in the middle of the theater's stage just inhaling and exhaling . . . I don't know, theatre? Pure uncut theatre?

Robert and Michael assumed the roles of co–artistic directors and opened their doors to playwrights, directors, and theatre companies with in-your-face manifestos about changing the world. But it was Michael's realm, and he had a new idea for a new performance piece.

Over his pint at the faux pub, he told me about it—his plan. He was going to direct an ambitious environmental theatre adaptation of William Faulkner's novel *As I Lay Dying* from 1930, a sprawling tale about a grotesque hillbilly family in Mississippi honoring their matriarch's dying wish that she be buried close to her people in the next country, forty miles away. What should be a simple journey turns into a slapstick existential odyssey. The novel is a feverish, country-fried tragicomedy told from multiple points of view, each monologue a peek inside the heads and dark hearts of Faulkner's characters.

I asked him how long it would be, and his guess was four hours. Four hours. The cast would be at least fifteen people. His brother would build a giant set—a huge box—and everyone, the actors and the audience, would sit in the box. The Box.

"How big?" I asked.

"Big."

"Big enough to fit everyone?"

"Yes."

It would be his most ambitious piece, and I could hear the hope in his voice. Michael wanted to be a serious director, respected by critics and peers. He wanted the life of Richard Foreman, the grizzled old art goblin whose plays resembled surreal dioramas crammed with strange props and loud noises and deadpan actors. He didn't quite have the rights to adapt Faulkner's novel, but he was working on the script anyway, and Darren was starting to measure and cut piles of cheap lumber. The next step was assembling the cast. Robert would play Darl, the second eldest child of Addie and Anse Bundren. The play was to run from mid-February to early March for a total of sixteen performances, four per week on Thursday, Friday, Saturday, and Sunday, with shows on two Wednesdays. Rehearsals would last about a month, and it would be an intense month.

He asked me if I had ever read *As I Lay Dying*, and I lied. Of course, I'd read it. The whole production sounded long and boring and doomed to fail. He was excited, though, and then he patted my knee and said with a smile, "You should audition."

Michael was throwing me a lifeline—casually, as if it wasn't a big deal. I think I repeated his words back to him: "I should audition?" He nodded.

* * *

I had been trying to resist playing games of "remember when," because thinking of the past usually led me to remembering unbearably happy times and quieter, more painful moments, like eating ice-cold slices of apple pie in the hospital cafeteria by myself. But drinking with Michael reminded me of late nights with the Legion of Doom a few years earlier, another lifetime. I missed hanging out with David and Michael, the three of us babbling for hours over plates of scrambled eggs or cans of Pabst, talking about what was important to us at the time: rising rents, the lack of public arts funding, Richard Foreman's newest stage delirium.

Always Foreman.

I first learned of Foreman because the East Village used to be papered with stark black-and-white posters to his shows. These plays had titles like *King Cowboy Rufus Rules the Universe* or *The Gods Are Pounding My Head!* and featured illustrations of severe-looking people. The posters looked like they were promoting an indie movie, not a play in a small theater.

Foreman had moved to New York City after graduating from the Yale School of Drama in the 1960s and was immediately influenced by the Living Theatre and the experimental film scene. He founded his theatre company, The Ontological-Hysteric Theater, in 1968 and started to produce and write and direct stylish, multimedia theatrical happenings. His work was idiosyncratic, an acquired taste, but that doesn't mean he struggled in obscurity. He's been celebrated for decades, having been awarded multiple Obies and grants from the National Endowment for the Arts and a MacArthur Fellowship. Over the course of his career, he's gone from offbeat curiosity to downtown elder statesman.

I was surrounded by people who wanted to be Richard Foreman—except Bani, who was too hot-blooded for Foreman's fussy living paintings. I found his stylish productions to be hypnotizing bores, but I never told anyone that because I wanted to belong. It was also easy to understand his allure: Foreman was a god whose actors moved and spoke exactly as they were instructed within intricate dioramas, and during these performances, Foreman would sometimes pipe his voice through speakers and recite droning gibberish as he pulled the strings of his young puppets like a demonic Geppetto.

Foreman's work flirted with cinema. He would mic his actors, so every breath and saliva-slicked lip smack could be heard. This was also a favorite Wooster Group trick, and it went against everything my voice teacher in college taught. And not just her: I knew directors who thought of microphones as signs of weakness because a real actor could project a whisper to the back rows. But Foreman wanted a theater that was more intimate, like cinema, without losing the unpredictability and humidity of live performance.

His productions vibrated with worry and yearning and, surprisingly, slapstick comedy. Foreman's staged alternate realities were crowded with obstacles and sounds, and his characters stomped around his colorful wastelands like fabulous zombies. If Foreman was political, then his ideologies were molecular, almost invisible. What was clear, though, is that he thought the entire human condition was a whoopee cushion, a funny noise, a prank, a thing that is not real because when you sit on a whoopee cushion, you are not actually farting.

To be like Foreman was to drag your dreams out of your subconscious and to push them on stage, naked, in front of a dark crowd of strangers. The directors I had worked with accepted that the theatre is controlled chaos; they all had strategies to subtly or not so subtly manipulate actors into doing what they wanted, and the results were always uneven. Actors are feline in temperament and gravitate toward warmth and food and their whims.

But Foreman didn't conduct. He shaped. Sculpted. He moved actors like chess pieces. He fiddled and sighed and got what he wanted just right. Just so. His theatre was like an installation that came to life for a few hours every night.

Foreman wasn't the only downtown theatre luminary. LeCompte's Wooster Group was probably more renowned than Foreman, and in some ways weirder. And I knew more than a few devout followers of playwright Mac Wellman, who had been writing unruly word-drunk stage poems since the late '70s. But Foreman was who my friends talked about.

Foreman announced he was retiring from the theatre in 2009, and then, again, in 2013. He's being talked about right now, as you read this, in some poorly ventilated black-box theater in Bushwick.

* * *

Konstantin Stanislavski's most famous book is *An Actor Prepares*, and I prepared for Michael's audition at The Brick by getting wrecked the night before.

I started my Friday night buying the cheapest possible cocaine at Sidewalk Cafe and then meeting with David, the newly anointed theatre editor and critic for the then-popular weekly magazine *Time Out New York*. He had gotten the job in 2000, and it immediately elevated him from downtown 'zine critic to a bona fide member of the established arts press.

I had not seen David for a year at least, maybe even longer? I didn't even send him an email congratulating him on his new gig.

At the time, a positive review from the *Village Voice* or *Time Out* could mean the difference between selling five tickets and seven. That magazine was an important marketing platform for Off-Off-Broadway, and to its credit, it listed dozens of openings and closings downtown and in the outer boroughs every week, including short blurbs and recommendations, way in the back of the book, and the editors sent critics to the smallest venues to review the humblest theatrical events.

Meanwhile, every few weeks or so, the *New York Times* culture editors would turn their gaze from the Great White Way and Off-Broadway and send astronauts to the East Village or Lower East Side to observe the Martians and report back on their findings. The reviews and trend pieces they'd write were sometimes condescending—"Look at these charming/baffling/adorable amateurs"—but every so often, rightly or not, the *Times* would celebrate a weirdo and launch a career.

David seemed genuinely surprised when I called him. He had left a few voicemails over the holiday that I ignored, and I had only seen him a few times since my dad's death in 2002.

But he wanted to meet up. He had asked me if I wanted to see a show—something with puppets—for old times' sake and I jumped at the invitation. I hadn't seen live theatre in a while. His weekends were usually crammed, so when I met him at a windowless shithole near 6th Street and Avenue A, he had just come from seeing something at New York Theatre Workshop or The Public, I forget. We had a little time to kill, which meant a round of boiler-makers. We caught up. I told him about Michael's new play and that I was going to audition, and he approved, although he cringed at the idea of having to go to Brooklyn.

I had his blessing. He bought me another beer/shot combo and politely waved away my offer to dip a housekey into the baggie of blow I had with me. He was on deadline, blah blah blah, but he told me it was good to see me and I believed him. We agreed it had been too long. It's amazing how easy it is to obliterate happy memories along with the painful ones. I was drinking alone because that was the cure I had chosen, and it was like the chemotherapy that slowly killed his tumors but, also, killed the healthy flesh, the untouched parts of him.

I missed David. I missed spending entire weekends stumbling from small theater to small theater, eating slices and drinking beers out of paper bags in between watching impressionistic one-person shows about the decline of Western civilization or sprawling multimedia stage sagas starring an army of young, strong dancers or uproarious, profane comedies inspired by hip-hop and kung fu and science fiction. The shows that moved us both were always a mix of angry and silly, some young artist from Bumfuck, U.S.A. try to make sense of this screwed-up world.

He once took me to watch actor and writer John Leguizamo workshop a new one-man show around eleven at night in one of P.S. 122's former class-rooms. This felt like the big time. If Lincoln Center had a younger brother that smokes pot, it would be the Public Theater, and if the Public Theater had a drug dealer, it would be P.S. 122.

The cruel joke is that critics are bitter, failed artists, which isn't true. The critic has a lonely, vulnerable job. An unpopular job. The job description is, basically, people will loathe you. These writers choose a difficult path because they are driven. They love art and artists. Maybe they're a little masochistic, but I'm not a therapist, no matter how long I've been in therapy.

A good critic wants to be smashed or lit on fire or catapulted into the ocean. It isn't easy to open your heart and tell people what you think. I mean, not all critics are created equal. Some write very well, and those tend to be very witty, indeed. Others are enthusiastic and the best of those write intox-icating reviews. The rule of thumb for artists should always be to read their reviews with one eye closed. You're never as bad as they say, but you're never as good, either.

The show was mercifully short. Afterwards, we parted ways, both prom-ising to see each other again soon. I watched David stroll north and I decided to walk around, slow and high as a tropical bird.

Walking is one of the only genuinely free things you can do in a city like New York. So I walked around in the cold, sucking down Marlboros, wiping my nose clean of snot, and trying not to step into hidden slush lakes. January in New York is cold and colorless like a drowned rat.

I tried not to think about the audition, which was hours away. Saturday morning.

The 9/11 attacks had been successfully transformed into a national myth and a political prop by 2004, but it was still a literal open wound to anyone who lived in the five boroughs. I knew a bunch of people who had moved away since 2001, convinced the smoldering crater downtown would swallow the island. But that didn't happen. In fact, what did happen was that thousands of young people flocked to New York, bringing with them fresh supplies of hope and want.

New York City immediately post-9/11 was still very much Manhattan versus the outer boroughs, which were seen as crowded, filthy suburbs by the casual elite. That prejudice was slowly softening, though, since rents were soaring in The City, as it was called by those who lived in The City.

And it wasn't just apartment rents that were sky-high. Opening or maintaining a performance space in once undesirable neighborhoods was becoming prohibitively expensive. After 9/11, money started pouring into downtown, including the Lower East Side, which would be remodeled over the years into a new kind of uptown.

There was so much happening on the Lower East Side before its slow-motion transformation into nothing but condos. It was where rockers and bloggers and bomb-throwers hung out and snogged and raised hell years before social media ruined everything.

Those were days of cigarette butts and skinny jeans and iPods and behind every closed door was some kid smiling, sweating, dancing, losing his or her or their mind on molly.

I was feeling sentimental so I decided to stroll south of Houston and say hello to all the dead theaters like The Piano Store and Todo Con Nada, the quirky storefront theater that attracted beatniks and Morlocks. I also politely greeted El Sombrero, at the corner of Ludlow and Stanton, which everyone called "The Hat," a chaotic Mexican restaurant that served pretty good enchiladas and cheap, radioactive margaritas.

The beloved local bar Max Fish was still open and full of motherfuckers. It had first opened in 1989, down there on Ludlow, and became the place to be if you were pissed off and fanged. The bar had been there before the theatre kids, and it was full of hardscrabble literary types—you know, they have expensive MFAs and pill prescriptions, and they're mean. Max Fish was mean, the Lower East Side was mean. Theatre kids aren't mean by nature, but we can manage the next best thing, which is bitchy.

Collective:Unconscious was nearby, a storefront theater dedicated to works by the broke and combustible, and Expanded Arts, where my first play had been produced in New York City in the summer of 1996, a one-act homage to Chekhov's *The Cherry Orchard* set in a frat house. My debut. The theater was so small that the actors could touch your knees if you were in the first row. Next up on Stanton was Surf Reality, a small alt-comedy space, a much-needed sandbox for funny people who hated telling boring ol' jokes. Over on Rivington was the old Theatorium, a huge industrial-size box that housed the Fringe Festival for years.

The Fringe wasn't the only theatre festival in New York City at the time. The Ohio Theatre was another downtown organization that championed new work, and its Ice Factory festival started doing just that way back in 1994. The year before, HERE Arts Center had launched the American Living Room Festival, which sought to elevate multidisciplinary artists working in the theatre. These were both oases of support for dreamers who wanted to create art on their terms but were open to talking to any fairy godmothers interested in producing their work uptown.

There is a thin line between a crook and an artist, and the theatre is full of natural-born charlatans selling trombones and band hats and fast-talkers who have a talent for shady argle-bargle but not art. Luckily, in my experience at least, most of Off-Off-Broadway was run by dreamers, which is the primary qualification for "running a theater," which is the worst possible business if your business is business.

I missed these theaters too. Dearly. There are two problems with aging: the general decrepitude and all the ghosts.

* * *

I decided to spend money on a car service, which meant I had to call a phone number programmed into my Motorola and tell a brusque, heavily accented man where I was and where I wanted to go. He'd immediately respond, "Three minutes," which was always the response: "Three minutes." Would the car get there in three minutes? No.

The driver would pick you up in a Lincoln town car with easy-wipe fake leather seats and drive you wherever you wanted for a flat fee, usually thirty bucks plus tip, from anywhere in Manhattan to where I lived in Astoria, Queens. It was an extravagance, but the thought of crawling home on the N train was too much to bear, so I spent money I didn't have and sailed home in the back of a car that smelled like stale tobacco and the sickly-sweet chemicals used in air fresheners.

I thought about David on the long ride home across the East River, away from all the sparkling skyscrapers on the upper level of the majestic 59th Street Bridge, with its mighty spires and elegant iron latticework. I hadn't meant to ignore his voicemails over the holiday. It wasn't personal. I had spent the last two years hiding from friends and family, drinking myself into a stupor every night at a pub around the corner, a hostile little bunker of silverbacks and off-duty cops and sad-sack alcoholics drinking away the pain of their recent shift. I could drink and drink there and nobody would bother me.

I got home safely—which always surprised me the next morning—and immediately fell into a deep undead slumber for a few hours before rising and oozing to the audition in the same clothes I slept in. My eyes were cherry tomatoes, but I was determined to show up ten minutes early.

The second stop into Brooklyn on the L train from Manhattan was Lorimer Street, and when you climbed to the street, the first things you saw were a greasy old diner, a sad little concrete park, rows of squat apartment buildings and storefronts, and, in the distance, the noisy Brooklyn-Queens Expressway, a massive and impolite-looking elevated highway that ate its way through the boroughs, like a rumbling concrete river in the sky.

This was Williamsburg, the new capital of broke-ass cool. This is where everyone ended up after The Great Hipster Exodus of the Early Aughts. Picture throngs of theatre kids marching from the Lower East Side across the Williamsburg Bridge to find refuge and cheap rents.

No one who lived in Manhattan had wanted to go to The Brick at first. Complaining about having to visit Brooklyn was a citywide pastime. I enjoyed kvetching about it even though I lived in Queens, a borough that no one ever thought to visit. Complaining was also free and just as much fun as walking.

For decades, if you were a developer that wanted to gut-reno a sleepy or poor neighborhood or even one with a crime problem, you invited the artists to set up shop and perform and party in the hopes that would draw young people and snobs and tourists from nicer neighborhoods looking for the hot new thing. This plan had worked out on the Lower East Side around this time, with frat boys, Wall Street suits, and party monsters with Daddy's credit card showing up in droves.

Williamsburg was well on its way in 2004. Soon, it would become insufferable, but for the time being, it was mostly locked steel grates and expats from Lower Manhattan wearing Buddy Holly glasses.

The Brick wasn't the only brand-new Off-Off-Broadway theater in Brooklyn and it wasn't the hippest, either. The Brick didn't have any buzz in 2004, and while its shows were listed in *Time Out* and the *Village Voice*, it was a struggle to get critics or the scene's coolest members to schlep out there. Michael and Robert were sweethearts, and if sweethearts were more popular, this would be a better world.

Other raw spaces were popping up in basements and garages, unsafe rooms with visible wires hanging from low ceilings and sensitive theatre kids screaming into microphones and gleefully terrorizing their small but loyal audiences. These small stages became temporary homes to new theatre companies with names like Collapsable Giraffe and Radiohole and Banana Bag & Bodice that resembled indie rock bands—young, disaffected youths with beards and bangs. These groups had fun pushing the boundaries of what a play could be or should be, and they had this fearless "whatever " attitude. Their highly collaborative, multi-media performances were often studies in contrasts: atmospheric and brash, immersive and alienating, a little bit scary but vulnerable. They were edgy—more so than the goobers at The Brick.

Three things are true if you run a small, independent theater in New York City that may or may not be zoned to be a performance space : (1) You are one visit from a fire marshal in a bad mood away from being shut down; (2) The toilet sits in an unventilated closet, and no dusty can of floral spray can mask the hideous stenches therein; and (3) There is a ratty, stained coach somewhere backstage or onstage, and everyone has had sex on it.

The early Brick productions were unpolished and easy to produce, a mix of eerie movement pieces and embryonic theatre troupes on a mission from Jesus to blow up the Western canon. Michael wrote and directed a play that took place everywhere but The Brick's stage—in the tech booth, the crawl-spaces, the box office. When I saw it, I thought, "Oh, he's saying something," and I just wasn't smart enough to crack the code.

The door to The Brick was nondescript, and from outside, the theater looked like what it once was: a garage. Next to The Brick was an unfriendly bar only interested in locals—specifically, working-class Italians who had long called Williamsburg home and quietly resented all the fashionable new colonizers. The bar's owners were also The Brick's pretty savvy landlords. They knew they couldn't stop young people from flooding Williamsburg, so they rented out their space to a group that would draw people to Lorimer and the nearby businesses.

We drank at Union Pool, around the corner, a large bar with a concrete patio out back and the expressway looming overhead. That bar would become the epicenter of coolness in Williamsburg not long after The Brick's post-show revels were moved to a bar across the street whose free mini-pizzas kept you ordering more and more beer.

There were other dives too. And then there was a fair amount of booz-ing at The Brick itself. The Brick didn't sell beers, in case anyone is asking. That would have been illegal. However, a can of cheap beer would magically appear if you donated money to the theater by stuffing a few bucks into a jar next to the box office. This legally foolproof plan wasn't The Brick's innova-tion. It was what every theater did because every theater needed every dollar they could get (to buy more beer).

I showed up to the audition on time—ten minutes early. I slowly pushed open The Brick's commercial garage door open, careful not to trip over the raised sill, and stepped into a long narrow passage that led into the space itself.

I was nervous about the audition. Hungover. I started to worry: What if I didn't get cast? I was surprised by how much I wanted to be part of this show, and work for free, for hours and hours. It would be a homecoming. I suddenly wanted, more than anything, to be part of Off-Off-Broadway again. So I did what any actor would do before his audition, and that's stretch and shake it out and hum and sing tongue-twisters while waiting to be called.

These warmups came back to me, naturally. I don't know if they actually do anything, if they make you a better actor or not, but they give you something to do when you most need the distraction.

Michael was sitting at a table with a young intern, some poor unfortunate undergrad who dreamed of being an experimental theatre artist, which is a very niche dream. Michael smiled and handed me my sides, a few pages of Faulkner's prose: long, slithering, winding sentences like cottonmouths in the water. I read for the brothers Darl and Cash, and the passages were their tortured inner monologues, and I made sure to lean into my Southern heritage. I spoke with a strange, aristocratic Southern accent best described as "What if Scarlett O'Hara was a vampire?"

As a director, Michael was nurturing. He was almost serene, and his suggestions were delivered playfully. He never spelled anything out. It was never "do this," it was always "what do you think?" Well, I think Michael would have made a lovely European, so good was he at the art of subtlety. Americans are always in a hurry, but our cousins in the old country prefer a nice stroll. To Michael, rehearsals weren't journeys of discovery. They were laboratories where he could run the same experiment repeatedly to get the results he saw in his head. During the audition, he gave me a few thoughts and was genuinely surprised by one of my choices: playing the country doctor like he was The Ghost of Christmas Present.

At one point, in a hushed tone, he told me that I'd need to memorize quite a bit of text, and asked if I was okay with that, and I lied: "Oh yes, absolutely." That's all he needed to hear, although he knew I struggled with memorization, partly because I was a lazy, moderately functioning alcoholic.

He patted me on the back after I re-read the good doctor's part, and the audition was over.

I knew I wouldn't get any of the lead roles, and Michael knew that too. He probably knew that the night we had drinks when he told me about the audition. Luckily for me, there were a few small parts that required actors to play multiple roles.

I still wondered if I would get into his play on the way home, which took almost two hours. It was one of those New York subway trips where everything goes wrong, when trains stop in the middle of tunnels forever, and you end up dying on the R train and coming back to life on the 7.

When I got home, I was hungry. The only food in my fridge was a single frozen burrito, and I tore open the box to get at it before realizing that, in a drunken fit of rage a few weeks prior, I had wrenched the oven door off its hinges. I had also put a hole in the bathroom wall. I had forgotten I had done that. Why did I do that? I didn't have a reason. Maybe I was pissed that I was out of mustard? Or that my dad had died? Or it was Tuesday?

I left the burrito to thaw on a plate and ate it in the morning.

* * *

A few days after the audition, I received news of two opportunities via two separate emails.

The first was a job offer. I had been interviewing, on and off, for the past few months at the popular men's magazine *Maxim*, and they wanted to hire me as a full-time associate editor. In 2000, I had helped launch *Maxim*'s website. That job was a fluke. I applied online and weeks later, I was being taught very basic HTML. I didn't work there long—six months?—and left to join an internet startup that immediately failed. I swore I would never crawl back to *Maxim*. Anyway, I crawled back.

Luckily, the cynical, cultured editor who interviewed me didn't care about *Maxim*'s website or any website. He lived in a reality where websites didn't exist. But he liked me and I was there because I worked at Comedy Central. And I had service journalism experience. I knew how to write about products, which was slavishly. The next thing I knew, I had been cast in the role of "Dude Hack" in a production of *Maxim Magazine*.

Maxim was an import from the UK famous for sarcastic frat-boy humor and putting B-list starlets in bikinis on the cover. It was both sexist trash and a gender-defining mega-hit that burned brightly throughout the early aughts, a manly bible for insecure Neanderthals threatened by a generation of women addicted to HBO's grown-up faux-feminist dramedy *Sex and the City*. *Maxim* sold beauty and youth, but mostly youth, because if there's one thing American men cannot resist, it's the fantasy of a brand-new car.

You can bet editors at august publications like *Vanity Fair* and *The Atlantic* despised *Maxim*'s success, but even newspapers like *The Wall Street Journal* and TV news shows like *60 Minutes* had fallen over themselves to explain why millions of dudes read *Maxim*, not that advertisers cared about the "why."

I don't know if it was the war or what, but those years were an especially bleak time to be anyone but a heterosexual white man, and a deep-seated fear of gay people marrying and loving each other openly was a potent political wedge issue. I prided myself on my open-mindedness, but the traditional masculinity *Maxim* had commodified was inherently anti-gay without ever having to directly demean a gay person. I knew this, but I wanted to be part of a hit. That's the point, right? In America? I wanted to be a winner. No matter what.

I also wanted to be one of the boys. The *Maxim* crew were all educated, worldly, but they were still delighted by jokes about gays and gayness. Anything soft or emotional was "gay." The color pink? Gay. Sober, non-sports-related crying? Gay. Broadway? Super gay.

I was genuinely surprised I got the job. I was surprised and relieved. I hoped it would force an end to my affair with Julie—out of sight, out of mind—but it also felt like a sudden lucky break. I was swimming upstream away from minor-league digital media toward slick magazines fat with ads. The internet was a fad. Print was the future. Those are two thoughts I actually had in my head.

I would be working for a buzzy rag that sat in racks in truck stops and drug stores all across the country. Forget pointing and clicking. I had been trying to properly sell out for years and here was my chance. Absolute power corrupts, but nothing turns a person into an asshole faster than a tiny bit of success.

And I felt like I had made it when *Maxim* hired me for forty thousand dollars per year plus benefits. Health insurance! And in exchange, I would write about the three Bs of modern masculinity: boobs, bacon, and beer.

This was a real job, and I accepted it right away. My soon-to-be boss responded to my acceptance by inviting me to a post-work get-together. He said it would be an excellent chance to meet my new colleagues, fellow editors and sales and marketing types. The magazine would pay for the drinks. The two most beautiful words in the English language to journalists and alcoholics are "free drinks." So I went.

The casual meet-and-greet was at a storied downtown tavern, and I nervously shook hands and introduced myself to stylish men. Some knew who I was, and others had to ask my name twice and wanted to know why I was there. I drank a few gin and tonics and told a joke before I left. Here was the joke: What do gay horses eat? HAAAaaay.

Laughter. I was going to fit in.

Little did I know that one of *Maxim*'s dark secrets was the organization's penchant for hiring theatre kids: we were cheap and creative and disposable.

For the next year and a half, until I was suddenly and unceremoniously laid off, I spent more time at *Maxim*'s midtown office than I did downtown, a drone drinking at my desk, editing short interviews with cheerleaders and carefully guarding the key to the infamous gear closet. Inside that closet were thousands of dollars' worth of products sent to *Maxim* for review and photoshoots, shelves full of high-end booze and Nerf guns, laptops, boomboxes, stacks of DVDs and comic books, and bows and arrows. It was a room full of toys for grown men.

The second email I received that day was from Michael telling me I was cast in his play. I was to play multiple roles in his *As I Lay Dying* adaptation, which he was calling *In a Strange Room* because he could not secure the rights to Faulkner's novel. Michael's email was warm and professional; I was welcomed back. I had to remind myself that Michael and Robert, Hope and Jeff, and the rest of the crew at The Brick cared about me, and every hour I was with them was an hour I wasn't passing out on a subway train to Coney Island.

The first rehearsal was scheduled for later that week, and I planned to keep my two lives separate. I wouldn't tell my friends, the freaks, that I was going to work for a well-known purveyor of misogynist capitalist propaganda, and I wouldn't tell the men's magazine guys that I couldn't go to this press event or that rooftop party because I had play practice. That's what civilians call it: play practice.

Two offers, two new beginnings. The good news was overwhelming, but instead of cracking open a beer or rolling a joint, I inhaled a pair of hotdogs with extra sauerkraut. I ate them on a bench in a park underneath God's blue sky.

The next day, slightly hungover from my *Maxim* shinding, I made the mistake of calling home. I don't know why I did it, but I was on the phone with her before I realized I was on the phone with her. She was shocked to hear from me, and asked me all the usual, appropriate questions. I could feel the guilt well up inside me like blood in a puncture wound—I should have flown home for Christmas and sat in that dark house without him. I should have been a man, a good son, a brother. I should have visited Texas, paid my respects, and hugged my poor shell-shocked sister, who still refused to believe he was dead.

I told her I was doing great. I was dating a nice girl, and I just left out the part where she was married to a man who wanted to hurt me. I was writing, and I had enough money.

I hung up before she could whisper that he'd be proud.

* * *

When I told Julie I was quitting Comedy Central she looked relieved. It was finally over, again—the whole painful affair.

We had spent the last few months trying our best to leave the other alone: I had uninstalled AOL's Instant Messenger from my large boxy computer screen to prevent me from messaging her during the weekdays, and we avoided eye contact during meetings. Our affair had rules: No phone calls. No sex. Moderate dry humping was allowed—soft third base. They were very Catholic rules, which made sense since we had both been raised Catholic.

I was not a believer, but I also had this feeling that Jesus was watching me grope her in the single-occupancy accessible bathroom. She had married her high school boyfriend, and I knew she loved him, and I also knew she was not happy. They tied the knot too young, and Julie was ambitious in a way he was not. None of that was my business, but I obsessed over their relationship late at night, as I slept alone in my bed.

We ended things semi-regularly, sometimes weekly. During one of our tortured break-ups, I quoted Emily Dickinson because our affair was occasionally pretentious. I whined that "the heart wants what it wants" and I thought that explained our predicament, that we had no choice in the matter. But "the heart wants what it wants" makes love sound like a piranha, just hunger and teeth.

I wasn't proud of being a homewrecker. I didn't want to be the other woman. I have never needed an excuse to drink, but wondering if I had ruined her life and mine drove me to the bar during lunch hours. It was all so anguished and adolescent.

She would leave little notes under my mouse apologizing for everything. I knew she didn't want to be in this affair. We were not together, ever. We would only share moments, bubbles of time that would pop. I wasn't with her but I was rarely without her. I thought about her and her words and her body constantly.

On my last day, my boss took me to lunch, and later, my coworkers stopped by my cubicle to say goodbye as I cleaned it out. There were awkward hugs, and jokes were told because you can't work at a place called Comedy Central without thinking you're funny.

Julie and I went on a final walk through Central Park, the scene of many a fraught rendezvous behind bushes but still in full view of tourists. We were over, again, for good. She and her husband had reconciled, for the time being, at least. We strolled like Regency-era nobles, dignified and polite. Our conversation was relaxed, and we chatted about everything except that I loved her, or I thought I did. An affair is an identity-shattering delusion, and I was desperate to pull myself together.

I could hear the guilt and confusion in her voice as she slowly walked down the manicured park's winding paths. She had been a near-constant in my life for almost a year and a half, first as a colleague, then a friend, and later, a sort of lover, my very own Marius.

I pleaded with her on the street to leave him once, and we both cried, just sobbed, right there on Eighth Avenue. She couldn't. She wanted to, but she couldn't, and that gutted me even though I was petrified of the "what if." What if she did divorce him? What if she showed up at my filthy apartment with packed bags? What if she found out I was a slob? That I was in debt and a drunk? What if she found out the truth?

I had been laid off in the months before my old man died, and he supported my desperate job search from his hospital bed. This was . . . June? 2002? Yeah. He wished me luck while wheezing, and I told him I'd see him soon, and I did, a few weeks later, only he was dead and cold, and his mouth had been pried open when the tubes were pulled out, and that was that.

I had gotten the job. And then, the next month, I had met her.

I remember Julie's first day on the job. She was my counterpart, a fellow hack writer. The department was growing. The internet was growing. I watched her float past my cubicle and sit at a desk behind me, and I could feel her smile and her nervousness, and for the first time in weeks, I felt I could breathe, like the noose had been loosened.

Julie was a special subspecies of New Yorker, a Staten Island kid. That borough is often forgotten or made fun of because of its proximity to New Jersey, a heroically uncool state. All the people I've ever met from Staten Island are warm, generous, borderline psychopaths who will fight you if you insult any member of their extended family. Is that a stereotype? Yes. It's also true. I used to refer to it as Staten Island of Dr. Moreau, a joke that Julie didn't appreciate.

She was part Italian, part Polish, and gave off intense recovering Catholic vibes. I thought she was beautiful the moment I saw her: she had piercing blue-gray eyes, dirty blonde hair, and a cute dimple on her right cheek. Her clothes, her boots, her makeup all suggested not-so-secret goth sensibilities. She laughed with her whole body.

Julie was likable, a skill I struggled with. She taught me the basics and I will now teach them to you: Don't be a snob. It's actually cool to be excited by new things. She was my first friend on Friendster, the larval social network that made it easy to stalk your crushes. The site seemed so fresh and necessary. How did any of us ever live without it? It allowed me to wallow in exciting new ways. I'd spend hours staring at photos of Julie posing with her husband.

Julie was confident and quick-witted. Her previous job was at a well-regarded music magazine, so her taste in pop culture was refined—she knew who to listen to, and she was the same about books. I didn't want to flirt with her initially because I liked hiding in my cubicle and avoiding eye contact with my coworkers. But eventually, after a few meetings and a couple of lunches, I made her laugh and vice versa, and before long, she introduced me to The Smiths, and I marveled at how Morrissey was writing sad little rock songs for me and only me. When I told her that my dad had passed away a few weeks before the meeting, she almost cried, and that moved me. I felt instantly bonded to her.

The surprising truth about losing someone you love isn't that it's a calamity, an atomic explosion that flattens your life. It's that, immediately after, you can get lost in the devastation, drawn to it. I spent months wandering the wreckage, admiring the blight. I wanted to kneel in the rubble and hold on to my sorrow like it was some kind of treasure, and I showed Julie my treasure and she thought it was beautiful and mourned with me; she mourned for a man she never knew.

There were times when we could pretend that we were just coworkers who blandly greeted each other in the kitchen, and other times we couldn't hide our lust. We'd meet in empty offices and, you know, feel each other up like horny teenagers. Our relationship was a melodrama, complete with us whispering "No, we mustn't" in stairwells and empty offices. Our cycle was self-destructive, but at least it gave me a break from the chaos of my loss. We'd disappear during the work day and then reappear, disheveled and stinking of sweat and bodily fluids. I'd beg her to leave bite marks all over my body because I wanted to feel like I was hers when I wasn't and she wasn't mine. It was madness.

And we also shared intimate moments of platonic affection, as if we were siblings hiding in the attic of a large, haunted Southern mansion. For instance, she threw me a surprise birthday party at work once, and it was a genuine surprise because I don't know how she found out the date; this was before Facebook was a thing. I hadn't told anyone, and frankly, I planned to ignore my birthday that year, totally and utterly. I ignored phone calls from my mom and brother and went so far as to delete their voice messages without listening. I was going to spend my birthday getting fucked up and blacking out. The party had a theme, which was "princess," and I got to wear a pink crown and there were cupcakes and frilly, princess-y decorations in the commons area, and even though all of my coworkers were there, all I could do was focus on Julie and her mischievous smile.

On my last day, once we returned to the office, with an hour to go before I was officially an ex-coworker, she gave me a CD full of songs and a chaste hug, and hurried to the elevator. The CD was a soundtrack of our wounded romance that included The Smiths, naturally, and The Cure and Radiohead and Belle and Sebastian and any music that sounded the way Dracula dressed.

She included tracks from two bands we both loved, the shamelessly melo-dramatic Canadian supergroup The New Pornographers and underground weird-rock legends The Pixies. And then there were selections from The Postal Service's classic 2003 album *Give Up*.

The Postal Service was a power trio: Ben Gibbard, Jenny Lewis, and producer Jimmy Tamborello. Gibbard was the lead singer of Death Cab for Cutie, the gooey, turn-of-the-century sadboy alt-rock group, and he brought that same upbeat gloom pop feel to the Postal Service album. Julie and I would listen to all ten tracks on our computers simultaneously while we wrote copy about new episodes of South Park, and in between songs, we'd send insipid instant messages to each other like "love this song" or "love you." We'd do this all the time. We would download the same songs illegally on our desktops thanks to the office's high-speed T1 line, and this was a kind of foreplay, the ability to communicate intimately with our backs to each other, listening to music and pinging each other. We'd do this for hours, and it would turn us both on at our desks. She included multiple tracks from *Give Up* on my CD mix, songs like "Brand New Colony" and "Such Great Heights," deeply romantic, infectiously melodic, beat-heavy songs about floating away with your lover.

I fed that mix CD into my big, clunky Sony player, the size of a pita bread, and listened to it on the ride home, and then I lay in bed and listened to it again and again.

* * *

In an essay published after his death, literary gadfly George Plimpton described heaven. His vision begins on a tropical island and includes a dinner with famous guests followed by fireworks and a speedboat ride to a New York City pier and a waiting Yellow Cab waiting "in a fine mist." It's a lovely thought, the perfect day. One that you'd live over and over, a day that you'd never get tired of. My heaven starts with a walk in Central Park during the early spring, when the air is cold and the flowers are punching their way through the mud. The leaves are green and fresh, and there's a warm breeze and the walk continues to a diner: scrambled eggs, coleslaw, an everything bagel, slathered in cream cheese and not toasted. Then the subway shows up on time and it's clean and not crowded, and I am whisked away to rehearsal for some play that will never be performed. It's just me and my friends, and we spend all day playing and laughing. There's a dinner break, and then more playing, and it's a livery cab home to a nice warm bed.

There is no better use of time on this planet than rehearsing a play with a group of people you respect and who respect you, people who make you laugh and turn you on, people you trust and who will share bites of their lunch with you. I guess playing with children is up there, but after that, I can't think of a better way for adults to spend the precious few minutes given to them than pretending to be other people, with friends. One of the many pleasures of having children, or spending time with them, is the permission they give adults to play and act silly, to roll around on the floor and to talk in silly voices and to act like the floor is suddenly a lake of deadly lava. That's what rehearsal can be, depending on the director.

Directors have a somewhat thankless job. The very best have similar skill sets: artistic vision, excellent communication and organizational skills. But to do the job at all requires a thick skin. The director's role was explained to me very simply once: if a play is a hit, it's because the play was well-written and the actors were talented and the lighting and set and costumes were exemplary, and if it's a bomb, it's all the director's fault.

I was drawn to playwriting because, traditionally, the playwright was the driving force in the theatre, at least in the West. The playwright gets to hide in the back of the theater and watch actors speak their words, and they get praise and adulation too.

A playwright doesn't make as much money as a screenwriter, for instance, but a playwright's words are sacred. That's the deal. They are not hack writers. They are the exact opposite of a glossy magazine scribbler. A playwright's plays are etched into stone. It's the perfect gig for anyone who has ever nursed even the tiniest god complex.

But New York's experimental theatre scene flipped the script on that pecking order. The director was the driving force behind any production, and the playwright, if there was one, serves the director's vision, like the actors. The directors I knew in college were part traffic cop, part coach, and part literary scholar studying the text and looking for clues as to what the author meant, and they were totally subservient to the words. They were sort of like priests that way.

But not Michael. His script was a faithful rearranging of Faulkner's monologues into a script, with a little rewriting here and there, a few cuts, you know, to help the Nobel Prize winner out posthumously. He was genuinely inspired by Faulkner's Dixieland fable but this was his show. And his responsibility was to what he saw in his head, not what he imagined Faulkner saw in his. His novel was a recipe that Michael followed when it suited him.

In a Strange Room was Michael's vision. He transformed Faulkner's text into something different than what it was, something weirder and more hallucinatory.

It took me a while to surrender to the idea that the director was the theatre's singular artist, a benevolent despot hanging actors like ornaments on tableaus from Dear Leader's dreams.

This way of thinking didn't fundamentally change the usual nature of rehearsals, which exist to serve a vision, whether that's the playwright's or not. I like to imagine that rehearsals during the fourth century BCE or during Elizabethan times were essentially the same: just a bunch of peacocks getting together and trying to figure out how to work together.

There are three acts to every rehearsal, amateur or professional. The first act starts with friendly chatter and jumping jacks and vocal warm-ups, followed by the director giving instructions, and it ends with a break. The directions the director gives can be clever or blunt. They can clap to get attention and then bark orders or motion for everyone to huddle up so they can suggest a game that requires the actors to pretend they're little babies and the point of the game is to illuminate something in the script, a beat, a line of dialogue, whatever.

Act two is blocking and choreography and breakthroughs and then another break, and act three is notes, and applause, and then everyone goes to the bar or home. The most important part of act two is when someone has a breakthrough. That doesn't always happen. The highlight of the third act is when the director gives a note that either is, or sounds, brilliant and everyone nods and goes "Mmhmm."

The first rehearsal is like a first date: you're nervous and excited and reserved. You know you need to project confidence but you're also needy and you know you know you're needy. I wanted to be liked. But most of all I wanted to be accepted back into the club. I wanted to be embraced and I was, almost immediately.

I snuck out of work before five to get to The Brick early. I must have inhaled two cigarettes during the short two-block walk from the Lorimer stop to the theater. I popped a few breath mints before stepping into the space, which was mostly empty, just a vast shiny wooden floor and four brick walls and chairs stacked to one side. Darren hadn't quite begun to build the set, but his tools were everywhere. The Box would be finished in a couple of weeks, thanks to a few sleepless weekends of sawing and hammering and drilling.

Michael greeted me with the official theatre kid handshake: a hug and a few back slaps, like a pair of movie mobsters. I felt like a former safecracker coming out of retirement for one more score with the gang; I was coming home because no one else wanted me. I didn't have a girlfriend, and my inner circle consisted mostly of fellow barflies. The great thing about spilling your guts to drunks is they forget everything you tell them. Oh, you could tell me your woes and they'd pass through the holes in my skull like pasta water. Real friends listen.

It had been so long since Michael and I had spent much time together, and I thanked him, again, for casting me and asking me to audition and for coming to midtown to listen to me babble. He shushed me, lovingly, and

THEATRE KIDS

thanked me. I told him I hadn't had a drink in days, and he nodded approvingly. He hadn't asked if I was drinking or not but he was happy I told him. I was handed a script, and the rest of the cast started to amble in.

First was Robert. He was dressed like the lawyer he was and his transformation into an actor was instantaneous—a smile, a hug, a honey-dipped, slightly ironic "Howdy." He was polite and genuine, and it's difficult to be both. Most people, especially Southerners, can't pull off that trick.

Robert was soft-spoken unless he was cast as a madman, and then he expanded like a cobra's hood and became bigger, fiercer, more dangerous, and with the snap of a finger, he could deflate, tremble, and reveal a vulnerability I never quite got used to. He was always there when I needed him, like when I fell off the bar at the hipster honky-tonk Doc Holliday's across from Tompkins Square Park. It had been my twenty-fifth birthday party, and while my dad was still alive then—barely—I had decided to try to forget him anyway. Robert picked me up off the floor, made sure I was not bleeding, and disappeared into the night, and that had been our relationship for years.

Robert was cast as Darl, one of the brothers who loses it. Next was Darl's mother, the dead Addie, played by Ivanna. Addie got a marvelous monologue where she revealed what she really thought of her family and the Bundrens and Ivanna would deliver that speech with coiled passion and quiet anger.

Ivanna was from Southern California but she spoke and moved like a New England aristocrat, one of those poised and polite matriarchs who lived in a falling-down mansion not far from the shore. She had traveled in her youth and spoke fluent Dallas and Boston, and you could tell she could handle herself in any kind of social situation. She was kind and accidentally maternal: I never got the impression that she wanted to be the comforting and supportive person she was. She just was, a natural talent.

Ivanna was followed by Alyssa, who was also cast in multiple roles, including as a horse. Another runaway from America's lawns, Alyssa was blessed with a tremendous ability to see through people, which I imagine comes in handy when you're an attractive actor. She was also a deeply cerebral woman, chilly, but it was a springtime chill—there was warmth behind her intense, searching eyes.

Then the rehearsal began to fill with the sound of small talk and winter coats being unbuttoned and bags being dropped. Michael had cast two other members of the Legion of Doom: Hope and Jeff, who both dressed flamboyantly, especially Jeff, who wore colorful button-down shirts every day, even to his day job assisting a pair of aging songwriters. Hope and Jeff always reminded me of psychedelic versions of the oddball couple Gomez and Morticia Addams.

Hope was from Queens, born and raised, and she had a laugh like a lighthouse, a loud, friendly cackle that sounded like a cross between a Halloween witch and Falstaff. She was also a gifted comedic actor, and one of her characters, a cranky old coot named Pappy, was for me personally one of the highlights of the show.

The joke around The Brick was that Jeff was "the thinking man's John DeVore" and that I was the poor man's Jeff and we both loved the gag. I envied Jeff's erudition and discipline, and I did my level best to keep that a secret from him.

Michael had decided that the role of the youngest Bundren, Vardaman, would be split between an eight-year-old actor and Jeff, who had predicted that his youthful appearance would doom him to play the character—the rambling monologues couldn't possibly be delivered by a child actor. Vardaman would literally be split in two, a child and a sort of ghostly man-child, for lack of a better word. The boy would play Vardaman when he was interacting with family on the trip, and Jeff would handle his confused, innermost thoughts. This was Jeff's worst-case scenario but he accepted the role grimly, like a loyal low-level gangster getting his marching orders from the don.

The rest of the cast included Peter as the literal-minded eldest son Cash. Peter came to The Brick via Lower East Side theatre collectives like Todo Con Nada and he was a wonderfully unique actor, a shy Vulcan who could turn his talents on and off like searchlights. I was joined in the ensemble by Danny, a sweetly cynical writer and friend of Hope and Jeff. Danny had a rascal's giggle and a connoisseur's taste in film and could entertain and make each of us laugh for hours.

Ivanna had introduced an older actor by the name of Lawrence to Michael. Lawrence was kind and charming, a natural gentleman on and off stage, and he was a welcome addition to the ensemble. A dashing actor named Chime was cast as Jewel, the smoldering son in love with his horse, and then there was Dan as the Bundren family patriarch Anse, a tall, older, gangly actor who would understand more than anyone that Faulkner's characters are gargoyles. He was prickly, but if the play had an anchor, he was that anchor. His performance was a first, and his intensity on and off stage set the tone as much as Michael's direction. He wasn't much interested in hanging out with a bunch of twentysomethings but he would, eventually, open up and talk to me about football, which I knew next to nothing about. But I was happy to listen.

Along with Alyssa and Ivanna and Peter, Dan was also a member of Actor's Equity, the nearly one-hundred-year-old union with a fairly consistent 85 percent unemployment rate. The union made it difficult for small theaters to hire their actors, even if the actors wanted to perform for free, and the existing "showcase" contract for theaters that had under 100 seats meant self-funded producers like Michael had to pay his actors' transportation as well as insure the whole production. This wasn't a boatload of money, except any money is a boatload of money when you have none, and there were constantly plays being put on that flouted union rules.

I was never a member of the union because I was never a working actor. To be a working actor, one must have discipline and talent and grit and I had none of those things.

And then there was a Mikki, who Michael cast as Dewey Dell, the Bundren's only daughter. Mikki was an actor whose day gig was working for a religious organization dedicated to aiding families of the victims of 9/11, a job that was close to her heart because she had been downtown when the towers fell, and saw the horrors of that day up close.

Mikki was from the wilds of upstate New York. She was the product of a diverse heritage, part Filipino, part Irish, and I think there was a little Swedish thrown in there too. She was beautiful and serene, and as we gathered in a circle to introduce ourselves, I was smitten.

She had recently been in an environmental production of Shakespeare's *Measure for Measure* at Show World, an old peep show and porn store near Times Square, which I had wanted to see, but I didn't because I had better things to do like feel sorry for myself or wonder if Julie was thinking about me.

I briefly thought about lying to Mikki and telling her I'd seen her in that production but I didn't, because I was a new man, a good man. Reborn! I was not an adulterer or a drunk or a shitty son. I was a member of the theatre, and I could be anyone I wanted to be. And that included a man who loved himself and who deserved to be loved by someone who was able and willing to love him back.

* * *

I had never read *As I Lay Dying*. I never even read Dostoyevsky's *Notes from the Underground*.

I loved books as a kid, but as I grew older, I found I had better things to do than read. Those better things included snacking on psychedelic mushroom caps like Oreos while watching the 1986 live-action movie *Masters of the Universe*—based on the clunky sword-and-fantasy dolls for boys that I was obsessed with as a lad—that starred *Rocky IV*'s Dolph Lundgren as He-Man, hairless and muscular, and the great star of stage and screen Frank Langella as the villainous Skeletor. Langella played the skull-faced terror of Eternia as if he had been cast in a prestigious regional theatre production of *Richard III*.

I watched this movie on VHS over and over and over.

Despite choosing to recreationally self-lobotomize, I still kept books within reach of my bed and bathroom. They were my primary apartment decoration—piles of trashy horror bestsellers and serious fiction that you know is serious because of its thickness and boring ol' classics, including Poe—but I barely ever cracked my books open.

So I bought a copy of *As I Lay Dying* at the Union Square Barnes & Noble, the one any self-respecting drinker knew had a rare-for-Manhattan public bathroom on the second floor, and I started reading it on the N train home. I decided to read it because it was the least I could do.

I took it to the bar, where I tossed back bourbons while continuing to pore over my paperback. There is a certain kind of drunk who hides behind books at bars, closely related to imbibers who write poems on cocktail napkins, and I've been both and I am sincerely embarrassed by that. My god, the mental image of me, brow furrowed, scribbling lovelorn verse on a sticky bartop like some kind of sensitive bozo. I thought Faulkner would have approved, though, that famous old lush, so I ordered more rounds until the words grew fuzzy.

The book opens with Addie, the mother, dying. Outside her bedroom window is the sound of her eldest son Cash sawing and hammering together the wood that will become her coffin. Addie has four boys, one daughter, and a husband, Anse, a blunt, scheming, selfish good ol' boy who agrees to his wife's last request, that her corpse be hauled back to her people in the town of Jefferson.

The Bundrens are a ridiculous and melancholy clan, and each member carries secrets and desires in their hearts and hats, from Cash to Darl, the family intellectual of sorts, a thoughtful and depressive soul who wrestles with big questions about life and death, and who slowly unravels mentally over the course of the book. Addie's third son, Jewel, is a redneck centaur hard as horseshoe iron, and her youngest is Vardaman, not quite ten years old, a boy who cannot fathom the hot, merciless world he was born into. The last Bundren, Dewey Dell, is a troubled, headstrong young women gifted with brains and ambition and cursed with self-awareness. She is pregnant with a baby she does not want.

Faulkner's novel is notorious for its multiple perspectives—the passion of the Bundrens is told from fifteen points of view. Each chapter is written in its own distinct voice, each slice of the story served by one of the family members or one of the neighbors who try to explain the spectacle that is the Bundrens. Each chapter is a new, squinting, watering pair of eyes.

The trip to Jefferson is beset with plagues that test Anse and his brood, including a biblical flood and shattered wagon wheels and a broken leg, and all the while poor Addie's body is rotting in the box. It is a bewildering and challenging read, and every chapter I slogged through thoroughly exhausted my two good brain cells.

William Faulkner spent his sixty-four years on this Earth drinking and writing a massive saga about the fictional county of Yoknapatawpha in northern Mississippi. He set fifteen of his novels and countless short stories there. He never got a college degree, but he won two Pulitzer Prizes and the Nobel Prize for Literature. Faulkner briefly lived in New York and spent a few years suffering in Hollywood as a mercenary screenwriter. He helped write a couple of classics like *The Big Sleep*, based on Raymond Chandler's potboilers, and one very mediocre submarine picture. But he spent most of his life in Oxford, Mississippi, the son of Southern aristocrats.

My mom spoke glowingly of Faulkner, whose prose she described as music—you didn't always need to understand it to feel it. I think she thought that Faulkner was one of those literary giants I had to know in order to be an educated person out in white-person society.

She found a copy of Faulkner's *The Sound and the Fury*, one of his many masterpieces, at our favorite thrift store in Northern Virginia, Treasure Trove, when I was a teen, and these thrift store excursions were becoming more and more infrequent. She sold me on the book, her eyes intense and inspired, and said it was an important work by an important writer and I went home with a collection of Charles Schulz's comic strip "Peanuts" and a yellowed edition of *The Sound and the Fury*, which I would hold in my hands as if it were a holy artifact, hoping its wisdom would seep into me without me having to put forth the effort to read it. That tattered tome traveled with me from Richmond to Texas, and then to New York City, and it sat in one of the milk crates I used as bookshelves.

My dad was a reader, too, but he preferred spy novels and thrillers and he read to unwind. He was a history buff, though, and had plenty of books about the Second World War tucked around the house in odd places, between cookbooks or used as coasters in the den. One thing he liked about living in the D.C. suburbs versus his beloved Texas was the wide variety of Civil and Revolutionary War battlefields and historic sites that were within driving distance, each an affordable and engrossing weekend mini-vacation for middle-aged men and mindbogglingly boring purgatories for their families.

I use the word "redneck" to describe the Bundrens affectionately because I come from a long line of Southern gentlemen, like my dad's dad, who would have been twenty-three years old in 1928, when *As I Lay Dying* takes place. He would have been in Louisiana at that time, years before the preaching business moved him and his family of six west. One of the few benefits of being from Louisiana is that you can look down on Mississippi, a hungry and barefoot state.

I am half-redneck. My dad's distant relatives fought for both the Rebels and the Yanks, and while he regarded the Confederates as traitors, he also spoke of how the South suffered for the sins of the country. I was informed, once, that racism is like casserole: every region of the country has its own special version. It's not unique to Texas or Louisiana or Mississippi, even though those places bred men and women who were particularly good at it.

I don't know if my dad had ever read Faulkner but he was fond of a quote of his that goes "The past is not dead. In fact, it's not even past." He'd recite that line as we'd drag our feet through the fields of Bull Run, the site of two Civil War battles, where thousands of Americans were slaughtered, a vast green graveyard.

I didn't finish *As I Lay Dying*. The script lifted and twisted and remixed entire chapters of text anyway. So I placed the book next to *The Sound and the Fury* and returned to the bottle as the ghost of William Faulkner looked on, unsmiling and severe.

* * *

There are few jobs where the boss is expected to lead like a benevolent tyrant. The first that comes to mind is the captain of a Napoleonic-era twenty-eight-gun Royal Navy frigate, and another is a twenty-first-century tech startup CEO.

It is popular to joke about the perceived uselessness of "theatre degrees" and higher art education in general because they aren't practical in the way studying law, computers, or accounting can be. There just aren't any public "poet needed" job openings.

But my theatre education qualified me to work in corporate America and, especially, in startups, and I have worked in my fair share of those unstable businesses. I have an inherent weakness for hopeless causes, and I've applied to startups based purely on the demented optimism of their founders. My acting teachers all taught me how to cheerfully take direction from emotionally unstable directors with big ideas who don't know what they're doing. And that's every startup founder I've ever met. I was trained to work for controlling people. Maniacs.

The theatre teaches how to get along with others, especially those you can't stand. This is an important skill and a highly underrated one. I learned to be part of a team and perform within rigid hierarchies without losing my identity. I was good at executing a manager's vision—even if that vision was "complete the database before the weekend"—and I was flexible, too, especially regarding direction. You want it this way? Cool. Oh, no? For real? You want it that way? Got it.

A theatre director is a leader, and a boss, and a sort of psychotherapist. After the first rehearsal, I swore to Michael I was going to stop drinking for a while and really focus on the work, and I made sure to emphasize both words: "The" and "Work." I used all the buzzwords drunks use to convince the people in their lives that they don't need help, that everything is A-OK, don't worry. I was "on the wagon," and "drying out for a few weeks," and "getting my shit together."

I was going to quit boozing for a few weeks, or at least, through the run of the show and that is my promise, my guarantee, Michael. I never really said "sober," as in, "I need to sober up." I had no intention of sobering up, and I wouldn't.

And Michael listened. Patiently, his mind jogging with rehearsal schedules and script edits and blocking notes. He had a huge binder, and directors love a huge binder filled with doodles and highlighted texts. This book—containing holy scripture—was proof of his authority, and he carried it around more than was necessary. One doesn't need to go to grad school to learn how to become a theatre director. It doesn't hurt to have an ego, but the only thing that qualifies one to be a director is angrily shaking your fist at God and shouting, "I am a theatre director!" That should do it.

Michael knew what he wanted, and when he didn't know, he acted like he did, because a director is an actor too. Some directors bellow from the back of the theater like Lear in his prime; other directors are so intensely trapped in their head that they shuffle around the stage whispering to themselves, and then whispering to the actor, and then whispering "scene." There are directors whose performances are believable and those who aren't. Michael played the part of the tranquil stage poet perfectly, and he was relaxed and confident during rehearsals, even if his actors weren't.

He was soft-spoken but firm. Michael had a talent for making you feel like you had his complete attention, and that made some actors take risks that he would either affirm or gently dismiss. He wasn't one of those directors who was very interested in the interior lives of his characters, though that's the preferred method of the established uptown directors. Michael wanted to fill his space with bodies and shapes and transport his audiences to a three-dimensional alternate reality. If an actor asked him a basic question like "What do I want in this scene?" he'd smile and shrug. It didn't matter what anyone but Michael wanted.

Rehearsal is work, but it's intimate work. It's close work, and not just physically but emotionally too. And another word for "intimacy" is "safety." In order to open up to someone—to anyone—you have to trust them. Michael made me feel safe, but there were moments when the rest of the cast didn't feel the same way, and that created some friction over the weeks.

Michael's rehearsals were long, and he didn't always use everyone he asked to show up. He needed time to get everything right—this entrance and that exit. He wanted to account for every moment.

He also needed space to work out how he'd stage scenes that were unstageable, like the massive river flood, which he solved by using yards of white rope to represent the waves. He was exacting about how his actors moved in and out of the space but not so much on, say, the regional dialects. The Southern accents ranged from acting-school perfect to cartoonish, and I had no excuse. I was just lazy. I knew a slow Mississippi drawl wasn't the same as the accents I knew, like the aristocratic Central Virginia purr and the Texas twang, but that didn't stop me from ressurecting my Edgar Allan Poe performance and giving one of my primary characters, the country doctor Peabody, a booming drawl.

But I still spent hours doing nothing. I'd read the horoscopes in the free weeklies, like *The New York Press*, and nervously flip my phone open and closed, ignoring voicemails I knew were from my mom. I wasn't drinking, though, and that was something. But I was bored. I'd smoke cigarettes with Danny and talk about movies. We'd stand outside The Brick in the cold and light one Marlboro with the burning tip of another Marlboro.

The "smoke break" was one of the most sacred rehearsal rituals, and I took every one I could. My old man died of lung cancer but that didn't stop me from smoking cigarettes for the next ten years or so. I tore through half a pack of cigarettes outside of my dad's chemo treatment center once as they pumped him full of poison. Smoking is deadly, but it's also an ineffective coping mechanism. He made it a point, during his final months, to tell me he knew the cigars caused his cancer. He wanted me to know he was taking responsibility, even if it was far too late.

There are a wide variety of actors, as there are people—actors of every race and gender and sexuality—but if I had to separate them into two categories crudely, I'd sort half of them into the "my body is a temple" group and the other into what I'll just call the "fuck it" group. The first group brings a Tupperware full of quinoa and arugula salad for dinner; the second uses one of the breaks to run to a deli for chopped cheeses and fries. One drinks lemon and tea, the other black coffee and Diet Coke. One gently stokes the fire inside them, while the other squirts gasoline directly into the flames.

But if there's one thing both factions agree on it is fashion sense. An actor's style can be summed up in one word: "comfortable." We are a species that prizes comfort. Actors are used to wearing costumes on stage and in real life, so when we get a chance to just be ourselves, we gravitate toward whatever feels good, whatever's loose or snug. Clothes you can move in or stain with ketchup. *In a Strange Room* cast members would show up wearing their temp job costumes, their rehearsal clothes stuffed in a gym bag. Sweatpants, tank tops, scarves. Leotards, baggy jeans.

Every actor wants to be a director or a dramaturg, which is the most misunderstood and unfairly loathed person in any theatre production. The dramaturg is sort of a literary advocate who serves the text when a playwright is not around or dead. There were actors who had thoughts about Michael's interpretation of Faulkner's cornpone opera, but Michael would just smile beautifully as they explained the South or so-and-so's motivation. He didn't care, of course, because he was more of a literary vandal than a steward.

Michael was open to suggestions and was willing to listen to everyone, but rarely took anyone's recommendations or advice. I don't think he ever took a full rehearsal break because there was always someone who asked him if he had a minute, and he did. It was like a royal court, with actors bending the ear of the king, hoping to influence a show that was proving to be long and arduous.

He made it a point to check in with me and ask how I was doing after rehearsals, and some nights, we'd stroll around Williamsburg talking about everything under the moon and nothing particularly important, like we used to when we were younger. I wasn't above trying to backseat-direct the show and so I'd pitch him ideas that he listened to with interest and promptly forgot. But he also opened up a bit to me, talking me through some of his thoughts on the production and the novel, which I still hadn't read. He was wrestling with the staging and the tone, and I could sense the doubt he was having about his choices. He was also overwhelmed by the needs of his actors, and his insecurity fed theirs. I interjected: Not me! I wanted to help him, to fix his problems, but I ended doing neither. Instead, I opened my mouth:

"What if there was more blood?"

"What if there were more jokes?"

"What if my character wore an eyepatch?"

I should have been listening to him but instead he nodded along to my undercooked suggestions.

I was happy to have the company and I think he felt the same way. The rehearsals ignited Michael, but the burn was hot and intense, and it tired him out. The juggling of egos, the constantly shifting scheduling. Endless logistics. The money. So much money.

Our walks kept me out of bars and they helped him wind down. I'd eventually jump on a train for the long trip back to Astoria, which could sometimes take an hour and a half from Williamsburg at night.

* * *

And then came The Box. Darren finished it without fanfare late one night. The Brick looked like Santa's workshop the day after Christmas Eve. It was a mess but a holy mess, and in the middle of it all, there it was.

The real star of *In a Strange Room* was the set, a giant box made from 2×4s that filled the theater. It was an impressive 12'×12'×6', with two feet of crawl space underneath. It was solidly built with slatted walls that you could peer through like blinds. There were two narrow main entrances that you'd walk up a few steps to open, two hidden windows in the walls that could be opened, a hidden skylight, and a trapdoor in the floor. The four walls could also rise, opening The Box up and exposing the audience to the walls of The Brick. In this configuration, you could really get a sense that The Box was a theater within a theater. On the inside of The Box, there were narrow benches lining the walls where the audience could sit—a total of fifteen, at the most. The Box is the closest I've ever come to experiencing what it must have been like as a Greek soldier crammed with other Greek soldiers into the belly of the Trojan Horse.

Darren had outdone himself trying to realize his brother's ideas. It was the work of a master carpenter. The Box was sturdy, which it had to be to accommodate audiences and to allow actors to storm in and out. It was also beautiful in a stark and unadorned way; it smelled like a woodshop, which is the smell of possibility. The Box was both practical and representative. It served as the abstract shack where the Bundren family lived, and the wagon they used to fulfill a promise, and the coffin where the corpse of Addie lay.

The Box also reminded me of the TARDIS, the high-tech time machine disguised as an old-fashioned British police box that is famously bigger on the inside than the outside, from the classic BBC sci-fi show *Dr. Who*, only The Box felt smaller on the inside than it looked from the outside.

To cram inside and sit on the benches for hours was uncomfortable, but Michael wasn't interested in comforting his very few paying customers. He wanted to confront them, and send them hurtling backward through the decades to 1928, to the Jim Crow South, to a part of the country that was poor, had always been poor, and would always be poor, a feral place populated by the hungry and the ignorant, by men who stared at women like meat, and women who knew that death was their only escape.

There was no relationship as important as the relationship between the actors—and their characters—and The Box, which could be converted into anything Michael dreamed up. The Box was also an unforgiving cast member; it was full of sharp corners and splinters, and actors started showing up to rehearsals covered in bruises from crawling through trap doors or sliding around on their knees inside, or just tripping up the stairs that led to one of the two doors.

The actors complained, but Michael was too focused on other details to hear what they were saying.

There are always actors who complain, and I was one of them. I do not suffer in silence. I suffer loudly. I complained about the length of breaks: I needed twenty minutes minimum so I had time to run to the pizza place with the good grandma slices, the one run by old-time Italians. I constantly complained about how cold it was in The Brick, and I learned to double up on scarves.

There is a popular stereotype that acting is the art of fainting on chaise lounges, but the job can be physically and emotionally grueling. An actor is part daredevil, part jester. The cast was a mix of professionals and non-professionals, but everyone was committed to the show despite brewing discontent with rehearsals. Michael's directing heroes were intense artists who believed the rehearsal process was a challenging journey of discovery and whose collaborators were actors who would endure discomfort and risk their safety if it meant finding hidden truths. The result—downtown, at least—was an acceptance that rehearsals could be dangerous and that danger is what gave those productions their verve.

I don't know how Michael could have made The Box less of a hazard. Maybe by sanding down sharp corners. Or covering the whole thing in sheets of bubble wrap? But instead of addressing The Box's safety problems, he decided to surround it with bales of dry, dusty hay to make the theater feel and smell like a barn. I have no idea where he got the hay. I think it was black market hay? Like, where do you get hundreds of pounds of hay in Brooklyn? But he did it, and it triggered allergies in half the cast. So chances were good that if you were covered in purple contusions from throwing yourself around a giant wooden box, you were also sneezing and rubbing your red eyes raw.

The bitching and moaning did not stop.

* * *

I am not—and have never been—a theatre professional so I don't know how things are done on Broadway or Off-Broadway or at any of the big regional theaters, like the Guthrie Theater in Minneapolis or the Signature Theater in D.C., but in every play I've ever been in there's always a mutiny. This can be a week-long campaign of angry whispers behind the back of the director or it can explode into dramatic confrontations between people who have dedicated their lives to memorizing and performing dramatic confrontations.

I suppose it doesn't matter if your play or theatre company is full of dabblers or veterans because gossip is often a symptom of a larger disease, and that's boredom. Rehearsals can be boring until they're not; it's not unlike that Douglas Adams zinger about how it's not the fall that kills you, it's the sudden stop. I have witnessed epic, Greek God–like emotional meltdowns during rehearsals, and I've worked with directors whose mood swung back and forth like Poe's razor-sharp, scythe-like pendulum. Truly, you never know what to expect during "play practice." It's like combat, only no one's life is in danger at all.

I have a theory about gossip that I have developed over two decades of working in offices. I have worked in a lot of offices. My theory about workplace gossip is simple: the amount of hearsay in an office is inversely proportional to the amount of work being done. The more chatter, the less work.

Those with too much on their plate don't have the time to blabber about the boss.

Michael's rehearsals were often exercises in extremes, seesawing between being emotionally intense and unbearably dull. The work itself could be monotonous and exhausting, and the breaks were never long enough. I was either saying the same line over and over again as Michael closed his eyes and listened or I was mindlessly puffing away outside, stomping my feet in the cold, and watching young hipsters slowly stroll down the street to the warmth of a bar.

The cast grew restless. They felt their concerns about their physical safety were not being taken seriously, and slowly they were beginning to doubt Michael's vision as it became apparent that *In a Strange Room* would be, at least, four hours long and that we'd be performing for the smallest audiences possible, since The Box was only so big. The actors were also having problems with their motivations, which was the kind of hokum experimental theatre directors despised. Who cares how you feel? Say the words, hit your mark, dance, you are a machine, a bicycle powered by a director.

Eventually, the cast stopped complaining to each other and began addressing them directly, and publicly, to Michael. They began to whine about Michael's directorial vision more than his bedside manner and The Box. Was it a realistic drama? A fever dream? A nasty little comedy about fools and predators, abortions and insanity? They were all good questions, and Michael struggled to answer them all. After all, he was outnumbered. The questions began to turn into suggestions. What if you did this? Why don't we do it like so? And those suggestions ripened into doubts. I contributed to the discord by rarely defending Michael's decisions. I would usually sit there like a wet pickle while they performed their grievances. When fellow actors would bellyache during break, I would nod along while slowly exhaling smoke through my nostrils. As I watched Michael navigate charming actors vying for his attention and second-guessing his creative choices, I was reminded of what Will Rogers said of diplomacy, that it was "the art of saying 'Nice doggie' until you can find a rock." I never saw Michael pick up a rock, but I could tell he thought about it.

* * *

I had not seen Bani in years, and I almost felt bad about that, but I hadn't seen my family, either. I had been avoiding anyone who knew me, or needed me, or had ever loved me, and I don't think Bani loved me, but he had a way of looking into my eyes and asking, "Baby, what's wrong?" He didn't always wait for my answer, nor did he ever have any advice to give me, but he knew. He saw me. He could smell turmoil in others and offer them the comfort of understanding.

Michael invited Bani to observe a rehearsal about halfway through the process. A very special guest. It had been a while since I'd seen him, but we picked up right where we had left off, with laughter and squeezes. He roared "DEVORE!" when he saw me. I noticed that the past few years had been hard on him. He seemed smaller, and weaker, and he wore a bushy, nicotine-stained mustache that made him look like a professorial walrus.

He asked me if I had seen the reading of a new play of his the previous autumn, as if I wouldn't have hung around and congratulated him afterward. I had not attended and I think Bani knew that, but he asked me anyway.

"No, sir, I didn't see it." I called him "sir" because I was raised in the South by the son of a preacher, and he taught me to be polite, which is a nice thing to be, to show respect to people you don't know or who don't like you, though being polite is also an effective strategy for avoiding conflict because Southerners love to fight.

I called Bani "sir" out of respect, and it always made him smile—partly because, I think, it would never have occurred to him to address someone like that, and it amused him, and Bani was a man who would have made a fine prince, and he had an appreciation for courtliness. I learned that my "sirs" and "ma'ams" were unwanted in New York City during my first week when I let a "ma'am" slip at a diner, prompting the waitress to sneer and snap, "Who do I look like, your fucking mother?" Never mind that not everyone I was meeting in the city was a "sir" or a "ma'am"; there were sirs who were ma'ams and ma'ams who were neither sirs nor ma'ams but a third thing, unique and proud, and so keep your quaint Southern niceties to yourself.

I was briefly honest with him: I was busy and stressed out, and he immediately absolved me of the sin of not seeing my friend's art. I would have lavished Bani with more praise, but he was there for a reason. He was there to critique our work, and Michael trusted Bani implicity.

"Come out with David and me after, baby," he said to me as Michael led him away. The pair chatted and then Bani sat like a Buddha inside The Box and Michael called for the family, which meant I could take a nap or read a book or smoke.

Bani gently stroked his mustache as he watched the Bundren family stumble about and bicker in various drawls borrowed from the movies and all across the American South. He even nodded when one of the actors managed to breathlessly recite from memory one of Faulkner's endless, sidewinder sentences, respectfully tweaked by Michael.

As the hillbilly pater familias, Dan's Anse was a shambling, hunched-over scarecrow of a man. But Dan's performance wasn't one-dimensional. His character was dim-witted and cunning, a quietly cruel man on the hunt for a new set of teeth and a new wife the moment he and his family decide to make the trip to Jefferson County with Addie's body in tow. Anse is lazy and selfish and Dan's brilliance was never judging the codger, even when he busied himself eating the dreams of his brood.

Ivanna had one, long, exquisite monologue from beyond the grave lamenting her short, unhappy life as a mother and a wife. Her turn as Addie was a stunner. Ivanna lent the character dignity and anger in equal proportions and the shocking truths the monologue revealed served as the story's emotional climax.

The women in Faulkner's novel are lonely, trapped in a life of toil by dishonest men, fathers, husbands, and sons. Addie's death was an escape, but it was also her revenge on Anse and her entire family. A woman is expected to love her kin without condition and Addie never believed that nonsense for a moment.

Mikki's Dewey Dell was sharp-witted but guarded, like her mother. Dewey Dell sees her family's journey to Jefferson County as a chance to get an abortion, and she has ten dollars given to her by the farmer she slept with to see that it's done. Mikki juggled Dewey Dell's innocence and her growing awareness that no men are to be trusted and created a character trapped between what she wants the world to be and what it is. Her Dewey Dell is lost, and Mikki knew that from the get-go, and her performance was probably the most human, and the most heartbreaking.

Robert's Darl was all shouts and whispers, and Chime played Jewel as a sensitive hunk, which he sort of is in the book, the love child of an affair between Addie and a preacher. A dedicated actor, Alyssa embraced her role as Jewel's beloved horse, wearing a long, brown wig and a corset, and both she and Chime choreographed an abstract dance that they hoped would communicate the closeness of their bond. It is a testament to both Chime and Alyssa's focus that their tango of man-and-horse longing didn't trigger laughter every time they rehearsed it.

As the oldest son, Cash, Peter, was as intense off-stage as he was on stage. He spoke in a warm, steady monotone that made him seem, at first, like an android, but after a few minutes of talking to him you'd realize he was a funny android. Peter was one of those actors who could just turn it on; he had an amazing ability to concentrate and play make-believe. He was like a faucet and when you turned it to the right, emotions flowed out. I loved watching him do his thing, and I have no idea how he did his thing, and neither did he. Peter just did it.

The boy was nearly perfect as Vardaman, wide-eyed and precocious. He didn't have many lines, but they were memorized and clearly enunciated. Jeff did his best playing Vardaman's psyche, whose stream-of-consciousness interior monologues were chaotic and hard to follow and blended reality with youthful fantasy. Vardaman has some of the most surreal language in the novel. Faulkner understood that the minds of children are as rich and perplexing as any adult's, and Jeff stepped up to that challenge. It was clear he hated every minute.

Danny and Hope played the Tulls, friends of the Bundrens, a pair of Christian bumpkins. I was the doctor who failed to save Addie and, later, I played MacGowan, an unpleasant and, frankly, stupid drugstore assistant who awkwardly pretended to be a doctor in order to seduce a desperate Dewey Dell. She slept with him thinking he'd help her with an abortion. This scene was made slightly awkward by the blossoming attraction between Mikki and me, but we were both professionals, or rather, Mikki was a professional and I was professional-adjacent. I aspired to professionalism. The seduction scene itself was successful because Mikki was a remarkably vulnerable actor, and I distinctly remember thinking that my character should take off his fedora before preying on her because that's what a creepy predator would do. The hat doff became my signature move. This was the depth of the acting work I did.

Three hours later, Michael and Bani huddled in a corner of the theater as the cast put their thick winter coats on and prepared to either go home or head to the bar, where David was waiting. He had gotten out of reviewing some play at the Manhattan Theater Club or Playwrights Horizons or

one of those upscale nonprofit theatre companies that plucked writers from
obscurity—they were usually struggling writers from fancy colleges like Juilliard or England, the country that didn't invent theatre but wouldn't mind
if you thought they did—and then gave their works lavish productions that
absolutely anybody who was anybody saw: mainstream critics and movers
and shakers and tastemakers. After these shows, David would descend downtown and, increasingly and reluctantly, into the bowels of Brooklyn to slum
it with his comrades.

David looked ruddier and stronger than Bani. I was happy to see him
and when he asked what I was drinking I immediately said "Jameson," and
we were well on our way to drunk by the time Bani and Michael met up
with us. Michael was exhausted. That was the first time I had ever seen him
so weary. I had underestimated how draining humoring a half-dozen actors
can be. Every rehearsal someone was pulling him aside to make suggestions
or to warn him that the others were unhappy or restless or stirring shit up,
and for certain, depending on the night, they were, and I wasn't above that.
I was part of the noise.

He listened, endured, and never compromised. Michael was intensely
self-critical anyway, and nothing we said was as brutal as what he could come
up with on his own. This was his play, and we were his playthings. He was
going to put on stage what he saw in his mind, even if that play was imperfect, and he was going to do it no matter what anyone said, even the tiny
voice in every artist's head that whispers late at night, "Why are you wasting
your life?"

I respected Michael. I envied him too. He was resolute. He believed in his
art so much he put up the entire $15,000 budget. His savings. There was no
way he could ever make the money back: the contracts Actors Equity offered
small theaters limited the number of performances their actors could appear
in. *In a Strange Room* was scheduled to run for a total of sixteen performances.

Even if we sold out every night, at a pricey $15 a ticket, there was no way he'd get close to breaking even.

This wasn't about money. His day job as an assistant at a law firm was about money. His theater, his play, his actors: this was about tradition. This was about standing in front of a fire and telling the tribe a story about family and failure. Michael wasn't going to change his show for any reason, but he did listen to Bani, who urged him to turn Faulkner's Southern gothic family drama into a horny burlesque, to take this great work of American literature and exaggerate it even more, and mock it. The ancient Greeks were fond of satyr plays, mini-satires that made fun of the intense tragedies that were all the rage. In ancient Athens, tragedians would submit three tragedies and a satyr play to spring festivals in honor of Dionysus. They were like after-dinner mints, cooling the palates of audiences who had just watched Oedipus poke out his eyes and entertaining them with disrespectful, naughty jokes.

I promptly ordered Michael a pint the moment I saw him. I was tipsy so I made a great show of asking for a club soda with extra limes. He noticed. As he took a sip of his stout, I told him to hang out for a second so I could make an important phone call but I smoked a wee roach instead. To take the edge off my sobriety. When I returned from my "important call," Michael leaned in and glumly reported what Bani had thought of the show. He made sure to do to it quietly—bad news is best whispered over beers. A few barstools away, the mad Iranian and David were laughing and barking and whooping it up. I could tell Bani had shaken Michael's confidence, so I did what any friend would do and peer-pressured him into taking a shot of tequila. The bar had filled by this point, noisy with hipsters and theatre kids, a gentle weekday pandemonium, and for the first time in as long as I could remember I felt held, and protected. I was with family, pleasantly, delicately, buzzed.

David asked me if I wanted to see a show with him again and I immediately said yes. I meant it, too: I wanted to hang out with him more, but I knew I wasn't going to call him and he wasn't going to call me. He was being polite. He told me to watch his drink while he went to the bathroom and I thought he was suggesting we do drugs in one of the stalls but, no, he actually had to go to the bathroom.

Bani pulled me aside and looked into my eyes. "How are you?" he said. I didn't remind him that he'd already asked. Bani spoke to me like I was a beautiful woman, with respect and interest, but gently, as if I were a delicate confection, spun sugar. I wanted him to be impressed with me, so I told him I was working for a men's magazine that made a lot of money. "Does it pay you a lot of money?" he teased. I ignored his little poke and went to brag about the celebrities in each issue, and he was not impressed. He was bored and kissed my cheek, and I could smell the cigarette smoke on his breath, and he moved on. I don't think I bored him per se. I think America is a place where the same songs are sung over and over again.

During the next day's rehearsal, Michael took a moment to check in with me before my warm-ups, which consisted of extremely light calisthenics and tongue twisters recited loudly. He wanted to know how I was, as a friend and as my director. His inquiry immediately made me paranoid: had he smelled weed on me? Booze? Bani had asked the same question at the bar. Was it so obvious I was rotting in public?

I could tell he was being sincere but the subtext came into focus pretty quickly: did I have any plans to self-destruct before opening night? He didn't ask that directly; he just patted me on the back and asked how I was feeling. He was casual but uptight.

I told him I'd never been better. I was enjoying the process. I returned the favor: "How about you? How is everything going?" Michael shrugged, mournfully, because he is an honest person and I am not.

I had attended my first AA meeting a few days after New Year's Eve 2004, weeks before I met with Michael in midtown. It was held in a small church near Union Square, and I acted surprised—shocked!—to find myself sitting in a pew during a weekly meeting of a dozen or so people taking it one day at a time. I would last for all of fifteen minutes, and I would not attend another meeting for seven years.

The first speaker started to tell his story. He had burned his life down; his family hated him. But he was grateful for what little he had, and he had very little: a room, a cat, a job cleaning up after others. Before I walked out, he repeated a boilerplate AA cliche: you're only as sick as your secrets. I guess when he was drinking, he lied a lot. That bit of canned wisdom was a splinter in my brain. I had secrets too. I lied all the time.

I was pretending I was sober but it was a mediocre performance at best. I had started keeping things from Michael, for no good reason. I had told him about my affair, and my search for work somewhere far away from Julie, but I hadn't told him I had quit Comedy Central and was going to start a new job at a literary journal for chauvinist pigs. I didn't tell him I was going to be between jobs, that my schedule would be wide open each day before rehearsals.

I suppose I worried that if he knew I had all this free time alone, he'd worry about my mental health. We're both natural-born worriers.

The night before my first full day of doing nothing had been spent watching Michael quietly, intensely make suggestions to his increasingly exhausted actors, and afterward, I decided to celebrate, which meant finding a watering hole far from judgmental eyes.

The cast had invited me out for burgers at Dumont, a modest restaurant with high self-esteem serving the neighborhood's growing population of creative outcasts. But I politely declined, preferring the company of total strangers. Later, I considered pivoting my bullshit away from "I'm on the wagon" to "I'm cutting back."

One does not "fall off the wagon," by the way. That's the wrong verb; it makes the decision sound violent. No. It's more like floating. So I floated down, down, down until I was happy. Drunk. I had promised Michael I was going to dry out and give up the bottle for The Theatre, but he didn't see me slither away. He didn't know.

I spent the next few hours in Brooklyn talking to a guy the size of a commercial freezer who complained about women and bought me a couple of rounds of beers. He had a theory: the bigger the boobs, the more faithful the broad and I swear to you he used the word "broad." In 2004. I mentioned to him, off-handedly, that I was starting work at *Maxim* soon and he bought me one more beer. He was a fan.

He offered me some blow, too, but in a surprise moment of self-restraint, I politely turned it down and started the long journey home.

I lit a cigarette while I waited to transfer to a N train on the elevated Queensboro Plaza platform, and I got three good puffs in before a cop walked up to me out of nowhere and ruined my mild, pleasant buzz. I dropped the butt, stepped on it, and immediately said, "I'm sorry, Officer." Did I know I'm not supposed to smoke on a platform? Even one outside? My "yes, sir"s were firm, clear, and contrite. I apologized again. Have you been drinking? Yes, sir, I said, a couple of beers. Where do you live? Astoria. I tried to look sheepish but confident and, most of all, respectful. He paused momentarily, looked me up and down, and told me not to do it again, and I exhaled. Thank you, sir. Thank you.

He walked away. I felt like I had won the lottery. That called for a celebration, which was a code word for more alcohol.

When I woke up, there was a voicemail message from my mom. She was returning my call. I had called her sometime between leaving my local and collapsing onto my bed, fully clothed. That must have been 2 AM. I didn't remember dialing her. I also didn't remember buying a slice of pizza, but right there, in my sheets, was a crust, like a discarded bone in a bear's den. Her message was brief: Please call back. There was a pause before she asked me if I was taking care of myself. Was I taking care of myself? I didn't know the answer to that. So I didn't call her back.

I hated my phone and considered breaking it into two pieces, like a crab leg.

* * *

I found myself with idle hands during the day as I waited to start my new job. It was only for a week, but I remember feeling anxious. I had wanted time off but then I came down with an acute case of be-careful-what-you-wish for-itis. I had long hours to murder. I knew without anything to do I would start to decompose. So I decided to write a play for the first time in years.

My career as a hack writer had derailed my playwriting ambitions, especially once I realized success in playwriting was a combination of luck, hard work, and an Ivy League education. If you lacked any of those three, you'd have to compensate with more of the other two, and I have never been extra lucky. These were the things I'd tell myself as I settled for making a living writing marketing copy and nonsense for men's magazines.

There are more strenuous ways to earn rent than writing marketing copy and nonsense for men's magazines. Those were perfectly ridiculous occupations that were fun at times. I got to sit in pretty comfortable chairs too.

But the time I was spending at The Brick had revitalized my playwriting fantasies. I imagined sitting in the back row on opening night. The curtain falling. Silence. And then the audience roaring my name as I waved away the applause from my seat. "Me? No, no, no. It's YOU. I do it for YOU." One of the allures of playwriting is never having to worry about memorizing lines or eating sensible salads for lunch. Actors sweat under the lights while performing, playwrights not so much. Like the masked Phantom of the Opera, a playwright hides in the shadows and watches from afar.

I felt inspired on the first day of my sabbatical and immediately purchased a brand-new black-and-white composition book and a good felt-tip pen. I would write a serious play. Eugene O'Neill, only not long and boring.

I walked to the corner Starbucks, at Ditmars and 31st. By 2005, Starbucks had spread from trendy Manhattan neighborhoods into the boroughs. I relaxed my strident anti-corporate principles when it came to Astoria's Starbucks. It was the talk of the neighborhood and a sign that the white kids were attracting fancy new businesses. Everyone went for a latte or a frappuccino—the Greeks, the Bangladeshis, the Turks, and the out-of-work actors who couldn't afford the rents in Manhattan or Brooklyn.

I bought a large black coffee and settled down at a table with my composition book and pen. This was back in the day when Starbucks played soft rock in their establishments, and I scribbled to Nora Jones's hip jazz-pop.

My fingers immediately cramped up. I checked the time. My flip phone said 10:30 AM. I got to work. I wrote quickly. I didn't stop myself; I let it all out. That was the secret. I was fearless, the black tip of my pen scratching on lined white paper as ideas for plays poured out of me until my brain felt like a skillet scraped of scrambled eggs. I checked the time: 10:40 AM. I did a double-take. Was it only 10:40? I could have sworn an hour had passed. And then I hit a wall. The words dried up. I had nothing to say. I re-read what I had written, and it was stage directions describing a thirty-year-old man writing in his journal at a Starbucks.

I wrote a sentence, oh so slowly, scratching it out. I told myself that if I wrote nonstop for at least ten more minutes, I'd buy myself a slice of coffee cake. I wrote another sentence and gave up. I flipped open my phone: 10:47 AM. I sighed and went home, where I helped myself to a few hobo mimosas that were one part vodka, one part orange-flavored Crystal Light, the low-calorie powdered drink mix that my local dollar store always had stocked. I mixed those concoctions into a thirty-two-ounce water bottle with a wide mouth, which made them easy to gulp down. I followed that up with a quick stroll to the pub, and a pair of civilized pints, before weaving down to the river while listening to The Postal Service, and on my way home, I found myself sitting in the back pew of the modernist Catholic Church that loomed over Ditmars Avenue, a few blocks away from my apartment.

My old man once assured me that Jesus listened to anyone who prayed to him. Anyone. Anywhere. At any time. The Son of Man heard you pray in Mass or during Baptist services. He listened to Lutherans and Methodists and Mormons. He heard you pray at the foot of your bed, walking to school, or sitting in a car. Jesus was standing by, the sole operator of an infinite call center floating in the cosmos. Even more importantly, he told me Jesus loved those who didn't pray to him. He loved those who didn't believe. I would test him on that. Jewish people? Yes. Muslims? Yes. Satanists? (I was, and remain, not ever as clever as I think I am.) He paused and told me, gravely, that He loves everyone. Yes, even Satanists. And you, he told me. Jesus loves you.

The Baptists and the Catholics didn't like each other, at least traditionally. The Baptists were jealous of the Catholic's real estate in Italy and the Catholics resented the Baptists' singing abilities.

And yet he attended Mass every Sunday with his family and sang the dour hymns and prayed with his eyes shut next to the love of his life, a woman who believed in such Catholic bunk as the Holy Trinity, the mind-bending idea that the Father, the Son, and the Holy Ghost are one entity, a belief that defies all explanations except for "have faith." "Mom," I'd say. "How does the Eucharist become the actual body and blood of Jesus inside me?" "Have faith, mijo."

It's not like my mom didn't question the church, especially its earthly foibles and leaders, and she made lots of noise at our local parish. But when it came to biblical miracles and other mysteries, her response was to have faith, which wasn't a magic word. To her, faith was like hope with a halo. She had faith in so many things while he was dying—doctors, new research, his desire to stay alive, even for one more day, to kiss and love and hug her, to protect her and to be protected by her. She had faith, but her prayers were not answered, and neither were mine, so I was surprised that I was in a church in the middle of the afternoon. I was the only person in the audience staring at a giant Jesus on the cross, so I said a prayer. I felt stupid, but I did it anyway. I felt like I was making a birthday wish, nothing more. I greeted the Almighty appropriately. I didn't apologize for not having prayed in a long time because He's omnipotent and would know I was lying. I'm sure He also knew how pissed off I was at Him. But I asked for a little faith. I wanted to believe that things were going to work out, that there was a plan, and that the universe wasn't just a vast meaningless void full of rocks and fire and bacteria. Jesus loved me but He didn't listen.

I decided to skip rehearsal. I was busy. I had insecurities and resentments to soak in gasoline and light up. I didn't call or text, I just didn't go, and maybe no one would notice? That's how drunks deal with their problems. They ignore them until they forget what they were ignoring in the first place. I ended up at my nearby public house hours before happy hour, determined to burn. I wanted to be ash.

The usuals were there: an old Italian woman who had been drunk since 1977, a couple of silly Irish lads, and a livery cab driver from Morocco who told me one of his talents was driving drunk and I told him I had a girlfriend like that once. His name was Hakim and he would drink in my neighborhood far from the prying eyes of neighbors and family. He lived two stops away on Steinway, a few blocks everyone called Little Egypt except for the largely Muslim, mostly North African families who lived there. It was a stretch of falafel shops, hookah cafes, and a massive mosque that wanted to compete with all the Greek Orthodox and Catholic churches that crowded Astoria.

Hakim was a Muslim who had tired of keeping his head down in the land of the free, so he started making a habit of popping into my dive and getting shit-faced. He was very loud and funny and mostly tolerated. Mostly. It's been scrubbed from the history books, it seems, but in the years after the 9/11 attacks, and during the wars, Americans were true assholes to Muslims or any person of color some flag-worshipping patriot could imagine was Muslim.

We were immediately drawn to each other because we had the same taste in classic stoner rock, like Led Zeppelin and the Who. We also enjoyed highly inappropriate jokes. One of his favorites was asking if I was Jewish, and when I told him I was not, he'd wink like he was going to keep my secret, and then I'd ask him if he was a terrorist, and he'd act deeply insulted. Why do you ask? Is it my skin color? And he'd deny being a terrorist, and I'd wink back at him. I'd then insist that I was raised a Christian, and he'd say something like, "I don't like them either." And we'd laugh, and the off-duty cops at the end of the bar would give us the hairy eyeball but they had punched out, so even when they saw something, they didn't say anything. Maybe if you said the wrong thing or looked at them funny, they'd stomp you into hamburger.

Hakim asked me if I wanted to smoke some hash so we went to his car and he packed a pipe with the sticky, stinky substance, and for a brief moment, the time it takes to snap with your fingers, I was drifting among the stars and I knew I was going to be fine. We laugh-stumbled back to the bar. I ordered another round of beers and shots. He put Pink Floyd on the jukebox and an hour later I was reading messages from Michael asking me where I was, and I didn't know what to do. I texted back "sick," knowing full well he'd know that was bullshit. Another round. Hakim and I got deep into a conversation about the war, and I told him I was almost a Marine and he laughed and shouted at the cops that I said I was almost a Marine and they laughed too.

I asked Hakim for one more hit of his excellent hash. He happily obliged, and I inhaled the smoke deeply and exhaled. "Let's drink more," I suggested and he laughed. "You're crazy," he said. "I have to get home to my family. I've got to get up early and make them breakfast!" I lit the pipe again before he could deny me one last hit, and I left his Lincoln town car and had one or two more drinks.

Michael texted me back: "Feel better."

* * *

I played hooky from *In a Strange Room* rehearsals for almost a week. Michael checked in on me after I missed my third rehearsal and then gave up. I spent one of those nights drinking Styrofoam cups of moonshine at an illegal casino in the back of a bodega and another night sitting in my underwear, stoned, eating a Domino's pizza.

During one of my nights feigning illness, I accidentally left my cell phone in the back of a Yellow Cab. I had been pleasantly drunk and sleepy and on my way to a bar where, rumor had it, somebody had drugs. Once I realized what I had done, I had to pop into a deli to break a five for quarters so I could call my cell phone in the hopes that the cabbie would pick up, which he did.

"Forty dollars." That's what he said when he answered. His offer: forty dollars, and he'd turn around and give me back my phone, a device I despised, and for a brief moment I imagined living a long, happy life without one. I lived an entire lifetime in a few seconds, a life of kisses and hugs, books and laughter, and long lazy dinners with friends. "Fine," I said and ran back to the bodega to pull forty dollars out of its large, battered ATM.

When I got the phone back, there were no messages. No voicemails. In fact, no one had called me all night. I sent a quick text to Michael, which I shouldn't have done because the best lies are short and sweet. "Still feeling sick!" I wrote.

When I finally did show up, four days later, I walked into The Brick and declared that I was feeling better. Hallelujah!

It's not like Michael needed me at the previous rehearsal, but he preferred the full cast to be present in case he suddenly wanted to work a specific scene. He knew I had lied to him.

A director knows, but Michael chose to show his disappointment by focusing on what was in front of him, which was the opening of *In a Strange Room* in two weeks. The critics would come during the first few performances, so in his mind, he didn't have much time to make perfect something that was always going to be imperfect. When I told him that I had made a full recovery, he smiled weakly and immediately told the cast they would rehearse the flood scene, which was my opportunity to take a two-to-three-hour smoke break. I was not part of this scene; it was a family affair.

In the book, the Bundrens try to cross a river swelling with floodwater with their dead mother, and it turns into a disaster. Michael decided he would re-create the deluge with coils of white ropes. The scene was chaotic with the sounds of shouting and crashing waves and the ropes falling through the door in The Box's ceiling. It was chaotic, but choreographed within an inch of its life. This was theatre, the creation of a flood out of nothing, using only imagination . . . and spools of rope.

Before the cast took their places, Michael pulled me aside and quickly reminded me that I was not off book and that I should use this time to memorize the handful of scenes I was in. He was polite but firm. I did what he asked and spent the next few days trying to keep Faulkner's quirky, dense, hee-haw prose from oozing out of my ears and nose. But I can't blame Faulkner for my brain, which is a broken old screen door banging in the wind.

I read and re-read my lines until my eyeballs fell out of their holes and rolled under my apartment couch. I'd love to blame the weed and alcohol, but I had always had trouble concentrating and retaining information in school. Back in the '80s, the way you'd deal with a fifth grader who struggled with reading and, especially, arithmetic was to sit them in the back of the class.

The cast helped me when they could, and I'd return the favor. I was especially eager to help Mikki run her lines. But it didn't work. Michael had a lot of patience with me but drew the line at me improvising Faulkner on the spot. So I eventually photocopied my pages and taped cheat sheets on the walls outside the set so the audience wouldn't see. I taped script pages underneath the set in the crawlspace, and I hid cards with my lines here and there underneath hay bales and stuck in various nooks and crannies.

This method worked especially well for Dr. Peabody, the character I played who had the most lines. He was an obese, elderly man, and I was not, so Michael staged me outside of the box, popping my head in to deliver my snarky lines. That meant I could keep pages nearby in case I forgot one of my over-the-top lines about poor ol' Addie Bundren.

It wasn't easy keeping all my pages organized, especially when it came to my smaller roles, some of which were very small, indeed. One-liners here and there. I played a few backup hayseeds who served to move the plot along like a cracker-barrel Greek chorus. The Box was a coffin, but it was also a giant skull, and I was one of the voices.

I do not remember any dialogue from the play, except for the famous phrase "my mother is a fish," a sort of mantra repeated by the boy, Vardaman, who struggles to understand his mother's death. His mother is dead, like a lifeless fish pulled from the river by a hook. It's a touching and frustrating bit of poetry on Faulkner's part, as he imagines a child trying to comprehend the incomprehensible. I only remember this bit because I turned the short line into a backstage joke: "Yo' mama is a fish."

The joke did not catch on.

* * *

The "yo' mama" joke did catch on with the eight-year-old boy playing Vardaman, who I usually tried to avoid based on the wisdom of the great drunken vaudevillian W. C. Fields, who warned against working with children and animals.

Michael dutifully followed the agreements we had made with the boy's parents, and the youngster seemed well-behaved, a perfectly professional pint-size thespian who was respectful to everyone in the cast except for Jeff, unhappily cast as a sort of astral projection version of Vardaman.

During rehearsals the boy would torment Jeff, who was forced to act as a babysitter without the authority of one. Like any skilled bully, the boy taunted Jeff when no one else was looking and was all dimples when others were around. And this triggered Jeff; it stirred up dark old memories and wounds. Jeff never lost sight of the fact that he was an adult and this oppressor was a little kid, but that provided little solace when the imp would mock and tease him.

Sometimes I registered Jeff's frustration, but whenever I saw the boy, he acted like Mommy's little angel, which should have been a giveaway, but he was a good actor. Their relationship got even weirder once they started wearing the same costume, since they played the same person. They looked like Dr. Evil and his cloned doppelganger, the diminutive Mini-Me, from the *Austin Powers* movies. They were identical twins, only one was half the size of the other.

During tech week, Jeff took me aside and confessed: the boy was mean, and Jeff hated the whole production and couldn't wait for it to be over. I listened silently because I didn't know what to tell him and I didn't know if it was appropriate to viciously shit-talk a third-grader, even if it was behind his back. I was also stoned, which was becoming more common. Later, after dinner break, I walked back into the theater and looked over at the boy, who was nodding along to Michael's instructions. We made eye contact, and he smiled at me slyly.

That's when I saw it. Jeff was right. Yes, I was high, but that kid was the devil.

Hope and Jeff had started a theatre company in New York City in 1998 when they graduated from Bard College. They called their enterprise Piper McKenzie. The name was the result of a word-salad experiment that stuck.

They had fallen in love in college and had been together ever since. I met Hope first, at a party Robert was throwing in his small Lower East Side apartment, and I clumsily tried to flirt with her, but she laughed in my face, in the nicest way possible, and introduced me to Jeff.

The plan was for them to develop their own theatrical work, and for almost fifteen years, this is what happened. They produced Jeff's gargantuan cartoon extravaganzas, each massive work strangling or subverting some beloved, existing genre, stuffed like a piñata with Jeff's demented dialogue, rich with obscure literary references and zany jokes.

Hope acted in these plays and produced them with her boyfriend and later husband, and she kept him from turning into a human Hindenburg every time they put up a show. He was perpetually stressed, and she had a talent for giggling through a crisis while simultaneously resolving it. They had plans for world domination, and I sincerely wish they had succeeded and enslaved us all.

We got along, the three of us, but we got along because no one ever brought up that time, not long after they moved from upstate to Brooklyn, when they cast me in an early and especially maddening Piper McKenzie production, an absurd collection of strange, comedic yet cerebral scenes Jeff had written. During one rehearsal I got pissed off at the increasingly controlling and nonsensical demands Jeff was making, and I threw a chair at his head. He didn't need to duck or swerve because my aim was pathetic, but he was shocked and, honestly, so was I. It was a profound diva moment for me. I was jealous of Jeff's talent and devil-may-care attitude about it. I wished I could be as effortlessly creative as him.

I don't remember if I was drunk when I threw the chair, which makes me think I was.

We were in a rented rehearsal room, and the chair I threw wasn't very heavy. It was a school chair, mostly plastic. I missed his head, and Hope moved like a hawk, staring me down instead of tearing my heart out. It was an emotional time for all of us, which has never stopped being the case for me.

* * *

Everyone in the *In a Strange Room* cast agreed that the 1920s-era costumes were one of the most professional elements of the show. They were well-sourced and -altered and, in some instances, designed and stitched together by Iracel, a soft-spoken actor with a mess of black hair who escaped to New York City to meet other people like her—casual radicals with dark moods and shimmering hopes—who were also from far-flung lands: distant, boring kingdoms with names like Fort Lauderdale and Trenton, places where very little was going on.

New York City's theatre scene was a junk drawer full of kids from the wilderness looking for a break, no matter how small. We're talking hairline fractures. Off-Off Broadway has always been like the French Foreign Legion in that it took in anyone, but first, you had to do whatever needed doing. It's the price you paid to make art for free. Hand out programs. Work the box office. Build a set. Teach yourself to use a sewing machine and whip up a bunch of period costumes.

In a Strange Room wasn't the first time Iracel had been asked to take a pile of rags and Fairy Godmother them into a wardrobe of stage clothes. "It's who you know" is true and Iracel knew Hope and Jeff. She had helped them costume their production of Polish playwright Stanisław Ignacy Witkiewicz's *The Pragmatists*, an obscure absurdist comedy from 1919, at The Brick. This was one of the earliest shows done there. So she knew all about that small theater, with its barely functioning toilet, sputtering slop sink, and lack of storage space. She knew better.

So I like to think she only had herself to blame for saying "I'll do it" when Michael said he needed costumes for his epic, possibly illegal adaptation of a Faulkner novel no one under forty had willingly read—for pleasure—for a generation. One night, she peacefully went to bed in the world's greatest city and woke up in charge of the costumes for a massive show with almost no budget. That's finding, repairing, and keeping track of dozens of vintage shirts, jackets, and pants for thirteen people, plus shoes, belts, and hats. And dresses too. What couldn't be bought or borrowed had to be made from whatever shreds or fragments were available.

Iracel spent the weeks leading up to opening night in a nerve-wracking liminal space between knowing exactly what to do and not having enough time to do it. She had the patience of 100 plucky kindergarten teachers. She was steady.

One of the only perks of toiling on Off-Off-Broadway is getting out of social commitments by saying, "I have rehearsal" or "I'm performing tonight. Call is at 7." Another perk is telling your inner child that you don't quite have to grow up yet, which inner children love to hear. Off-Off-Broadway is one of the only places where adult humans, fully functioning members of society, can wear cardboard boxes on their heads, hold aloft a golf club like a sword, and declare themselves King Arthur in front of other adult humans, including, possibly, a critic from a major metropolitan newspaper.

It's fairly common to feel judged by nine-to-fivers when you tell them you spend your free time gracing Off-Off-Broadway stages. The follow-up question is almost always, "But what do you do?" Which is another way to say, "How do you pay your rent?" Oh, roommates? Astoria? Two jobs? Americans crave entertainment. We want to be distracted from the grind but distrust artists, or anyone else having a good time. Our culture only respects money and not much else. The father of a woman I dated for a few months, a pleasant enough normie who was senior vice president of something for a multinational conglomerate, once asked me with genuine interest about my experiences Off-Broadway and when I corrected him—*Off*-Off-Broadway— he changed the topic.

But when you're part of Off-Off-Broadway, you can wear glitter, feathers, and duct tape and be taken seriously, such is the full splendor and majesty of DIY experimental no-audience broke-ass theatre. Broadway is where you go for actors dressed like cats or lion kings, and way, way downtown, Off-Off-Broadway is where you go to ride your imagination like an exercise bike.

Michael wanted quality costumes. And he got them. Most thrifty Off-Off-Broadway companies don't bother with costumes, preferring black turtle-necks, street clothes, or trash. Actual trash.

The first time I fully realized I was in a real play that would be seen and reviewed was when Iracel measured my waist and inseam. The overalls she gave me made me feel like I was a proper redneck. Off-Off-Broadway isn't known for its production values, but Michael had a vision. *In a Strange Room* needed to be the best it could be, even though it would last for just a few weeks before disappearing forever.

The Box was impressive, a little terrifying, a Transformer made of lumber. The lighting was amazing and helped transform The Box, shining through the set's slots and casting eerie shadows. The lights could turn The Box into heaven or hell. But the costumes grounded the show, giving the production a tactility that it needed, and the performances were more textured as a result, all thanks to the skills and ingenuity of Iracel, who always looked worn out.

* * *

There are dozens of acting schools and hundreds of coaches in a city like New York. A few of these schools are highly prestigious, like the Actor's Studio and HB Studio, where legendary actor and teacher Uta Hagen taught for decades. But for every Lee Strasberg Theatre and Film Institute offering actors a chance to hone their skills, there were smaller schools that were cheaper and easier to get into, and a few were predatory, selling the promise of fame and fortune.

And then there were the coaches, mostly actors who were out of work, which is their natural state. Again, the quality of their utility varied—some were actual coaches, helping their students to grow or sharpen their talents, and some were garden-variety monsters, parasites, and sociopaths feeding on youth and hope or just torturing the vulnerable for fun.

Most, I think, just needed a paycheck in between gigs.

And the one thing this entire ecosystem had in common was dedication to some kind of orthodoxy. No one was winging it. Everyone had an acting theory, either derived from one of the greats like Strasberg or invented out of the blue, and I will tell you that it is extremely easy and potentially lucrative to come up with an acting theory. Every acting teacher in my college theatre program was working on a theory they could turn into a self-published book. The lines between acting theory and self-help program and religion are thin.

Thanks to my BFA, I avoided all post-college acting schools and coaches. I was constantly being told by actors with coaching businesses after shows and at bars that I needed to stay up-to-date on new acting techniques, but I always politely refused, except for Bani, whose classes weren't about what actors thought or felt. He had no interest in psychology or motives. He believed in the body and the voice and the life force, everything was sexual and holy, and those two words were the same. Bani's God was horny. The word made gooseflesh.

If I taught acting, I would teach one thing: how to memorize your lines. That's it. It would be a one-hour class at most, and I would charge an exorbitant amount. But I would never teach acting because I am not a good actor or teacher.

All you need to know, I think, is how to "get off book," as they say in the biz. The best actors—the most successful—know intuitively that brute force is the most effective way to memorize your lines. The best actors aren't always the most talented. Talent doesn't guarantee success, and that's true in any industry. Ambition counts just as much, if not more.

The best actors are also driven, disciplined. They want it, and they want it bad. Some of the most talented people I've ever known didn't want it: they didn't want to act, preferring careers in nursing or teaching or law. What you're good at and what you're passionate about aren't always the same thing.

The best actors are good listeners. The stereotype is that actors are self-absorbed, which can be true but isn't always the case. We currently live in a Golden Age of narcissism anyway. Everyone's self-absorbed. But even divas know that acting is a conversation, a back-and-forth, a game of catch. Listening is a skill society doesn't value, but genuinely blessed actors know that it is one of the secrets to the whole thing—focusing, breathing, listening to your scene partner, your audience, your inner voice. Insecure actors fear silence and pauses and almost always worry about their lines while waiting for their cue, their chance to talk. The pros listen deeply, inhale, exhale, and react to whatever is being said and felt.

They're also good at memorizing their lines. I've known actors who can read a page a couple of times, and then they have it, and I've known actors who lock themselves in a room and spend hours with the script, just hours and hours, memorizing. They'll read the script aloud, write it out, or record themselves reading it and replay it while they exercise or sleep. They know there are no shortcuts; you just repeat the words until they're stitched into the wet meat of your brain.

The very best actors can act and memorize their lines, and I can't do either.

I am terrible at memorizing lines. If I had a gift for memorizing, I'd still be a barely tolerable actor, but the one-two punch meant I was not destined to tread the boards, as they say. This wasn't a surprise to me, and I don't like to think it surprised Michael. I had struggled with my lines in *Notes from the Underground*, and I would get multiple lines wrong almost every night, but I could still memorize most of them. That show had been Robert's, so he was able to cover up my missed cues and garbled line readings. Maybe I preferred Dostoyevsky to Faulkner? I don't know.

The entire *In a Strange Room* cast were able to hold Faulkner's gravy-smothered words in their noggins, and I imagine it's because they put in the hours. Even those who were able to memorize text easily did their homework.

Michael was too overwhelmed by the slow march to opening night to care about my creative processes; he allowed me my shortcuts so long as I showed up on time, got into my costume, and hit my marks. He was so consumed with the production he had no time to go on walks with me, choosing to stay at The Brick long after rehearsal was over to putter and futz and work out blocking problems.

He was stressed and didn't have time to babysit me. I didn't take it personally. For the next few nights, I dutifully went home, emotionally ate Chinese food, and fell asleep reading my lines.

I tried to be an actor. I just didn't have it. I wasn't particularly talented. I also loathed the toil. The applause? That was pretty wonderful, but the amount of donkey work required to get to the curtain call? Not worth it.

I wasn't an actor. This was clear. I didn't know if I was a playwright yet, either. I wasn't a journalist. I knew journalists who called City Hall and wrote about grown-up things like Wall Street and that wasn't me. No. I started asking myself the most clichéd question possible: Who am I? I annoyed myself by asking. It was more Hamlet bullshit. Princely navel-gazing. Who am I? Fuck if I knew. Was I a friend? A brother? A son?

I used to momentarily soothe my tedious existential crises with a game I unofficially called "What If I Moved Away?" What if I moved far away from New York City and the cares and concerns of other people? Moved somewhere tropical, grew a mustache, got a new phone number that I never shared? Why, I could drink myself unconscious every night and never have to ask myself who I was. Because who would care?

III
THE SHOW MUST GO ON

I didn't fully understand my old man's devotion to the army until his funeral, which was held at Fort Sam Houston National Cemetery, just outside San Antonio. This was the summer of 2002. July. It would be my last visit to Texas for a long, long time.

He wanted a full-dress military funeral, and it was quite a performance —soldiers in uniform, baking in the Texas sun, performing a complex, choreographed ritual that included folding an American flag into a triangle and presenting it to my mother and saluting my dad with blanks fired from rifles. I had no emotional connection to the army, but here they were, strangers, honoring a man they did not know and supporting his family during their grief. My mom would later mention the streaks of tears down one of the soldier's faces, and I almost corrected her: it had been sweat. The day was hot— their uniforms were wool. But she wanted to believe these young men were wounded by his passing, and who is to say those weren't tears? Who knows what the soldier who handed her the flag was thinking about? Lunch? He didn't break character, though: he looked solemn, and if I didn't know better, I'd say he was aware of the streaks of perspiration running down his cheeks.

If there is one thing the theatre teaches, it's that fake tears can be as comforting and moving as real ones. In college, I once glimpsed the lead of a play poke his eyes with his fingers backstage to trigger waterworks. Once his eyes were nice and red, he stumbled back on stage, crying and raging and, you know, acting.

I was initially bothered when I learned he wanted to be buried in a military cemetery. It meant my mom couldn't be laid to rest next to him, which is what I thought she wanted. She never told me she wanted that, of course. I just assumed. To lay next to him for all eternity. Personally, I thought it would be more convenient to visit two graves in one cemetery but I was not consulted.

As we slowly walked away from the tent where the ceremony occurred, I thought, "Well, that was a good show."

* * *

My mom was named after Verdi's 1871 opera *Aida*, a soaring tragedy about war and loyalty and the doomed romance between a victorious Egyptian general and his captive, an Ethiopian princess. She exposed me to classical music when I was tall enough to fall over, long before it was the trendy parental thing to do.

We'd listen to booming, dramatic Beethoven and graceful Mozart and Chopin on vinyl, the record scratches and pops joining the violins and bassoons. But we also listened to mariachi music and, most of all, rock and roll: Otis Redding, Roy Orbison, Fats Domino. I remember pretending to cover my ears when, randomly, after dinner, he'd start singing Domino's biggest hit, "Blueberry Hill," to her. It was one of my mom's favorite songs, sad and sexy.

My dad had a nice voice honed during years of singing in his dad's church. A smooth tenor with tiny cracks in it. He'd serenade her, and she'd blush. Sometimes they'd sexy-dance and it was mortifying.

I shrieked with laughter whenever they did it. She'd wink at me.

Dad was gently jealous of the relationship my mom and I had when it came to the things we were mutually obsessed with, the books and music and movies. And she had superb taste in movies. I was raised on actor Charles Laughton's only directorial feature, *The Night of the Hunter*, a stylish horror movie about a murderous preacher hunting a pair of children; and the kindhearted racial fairytale *Lilies of the Field* starring Sidney Poitier as a Baptist carpenter who finds himself building a church for a trio of stern German nuns in the New Mexico desert; and *The Terminator*, a violent action movie about a time-traveling robot assassin.

She wasn't the one who sobbed when I left home for college. My real graduation gift was her letting me go as if I were a fabulous bird. She believed it was her right as a Mexican-American woman to decide which children were allowed to join the world and which would stay close to home and la familia. She would say these things and then follow up with a half-hearted "I'm just kidding, mijo," but was she? Yes? No? Both?

My mom didn't want to get in the way of my plan or her plan for me, which was that I give myself the chance to chase a dream, even if it wasn't practical. She was supportive of my writing and acting but would also follow up any cheerleading with, "You know, being a janitor is honest work." Which it is, and I believe that because there were janitors on my mom's side of the family; someone had to clean the big schools and hospitals and office buildings in El Paso. It was honest work, but I was lazy, and I had dreams.

She changed once he got sick. Their love affair ended five years after he was diagnosed with a lung tumor, and she fought that disease with him every minute of the day. She crawled into his hospital bed in the ICU one last time when he fell into the coma and whispered things in his ear and when she crawled back out, she was different, smaller, drained. I couldn't bear to see her so weak and human, and I ran away from her and my brother and my sister as fast as I could. I ran across the country to a concrete city surrounded by rivers and harbors and the ocean. I ran away and drank and forgot about him and my family,

The second act of *Aida* starts with the "Triumphal March," a famous operatic fanfare that's full of horns announcing the victory of the Egyptians over the Ethiopians, and there were Sundays after church when it would play loudly as she cooked lunchtime huevos rancheros in the kitchen. I like to imagine that jubilant, imperial anthem was playing as she shuffled off the plane at LaGuardia, anxious and worried.

That's how I like to picture it in my head because I physically wasn't there to meet her, or hail a cab for her, or carry her suitcase to the hotel she had booked because she didn't want to impose on me, which I was grateful for because I hadn't cleaned. I had just thought about it.

I was shocked she was visiting me. I was also annoyed because I would have preferred my family just to leave me alone forever. I was busy. I had things to do and drink and snort, and maybe if I didn't see them or talk to them, I could pretend that everything was the way it used to be before his sickness and that I'd come home for Christmas a big successful magazine editor and he'd be proud that I found a way.

But she showed up. I don't think she wanted to, but she did.

I hadn't talked to my sister because she laughed like our father, loudly and often, and I had barely talked to my older brother, the Marine, before the cancer. He had his own family and life, and we had almost nothing in common, except that I still held on to a fourth-grade fantasy that he flew attack helicopters on secret missions for the government, a tale I'd tell and perform for my friends during recess.

I hadn't talked to my younger brother either, not for months. He was five years younger than me, and we never really got along, except for that one time when I was nine, and my friends and I were roughhousing in the backyard, and Chris thought they were hurting me, and here came an enraged four-year-old hurtling at one of the boys and tackling him.

The family had waited until I arrived to make the decision to take him off life support, and he was dead forty-five minutes later. From the moment I touched down in Austin until I had snuck back into the ICU to pinch my dead dad's toe to make sure he was truly gone, just a few hours had elapsed, and I was bloodless and confused, and my little brother held my hand and led me to his car and drove me home. He played a song by a banjo player I had never heard named Bela Fleck. The song is called "Big Country," I think, and it was hopeful, the way a sunrise is hopeful. When we got home, he ordered a pizza, and we watched movies as the house slowly filled with family and friends and neighbors bearing barbecue brisket.

Chris and I hadn't spoken during our father's illness, but on the rare occasions I'd show up, he'd take me to the firing range, and we'd rent 9mm Glocks and unload dozens of rounds into targets, including fun, popular targets with Osama Bin Laden's face on them. I despised Texas growing up, even though I was raised to think of it as the Promised Land. In my imagination, Texas was Hades, an unwelcoming barbarian kingdom that was the polar opposite of New York City, and I have held on to that prejudice for my entire life. Texas was the land of the alpha cowboy and the Bible-thumping gun nut, but I found blowing holes in Osama Bin Laden's face oddly comforting, and preferable to listening to my dad wheeze while he napped. Normally, the neckbeards at the gun store would have sneered at my New York City ID, but during the winter of 2002, they gave me a Bin Laden target for free, and I've always thought that was sweet.

My brother cared for me as best he could, and I never returned the favor.

* * *

I don't know what she saw when I met her in the lobby of the expensive hotel she couldn't afford. This was a rescue mission and she had made the reservation not knowing what to expect. I knew, the moment I laid eyes on her, that I should have asked her to stay with me in Queens.

The thing about 2004 is there are so few photos of it compared to right now. I have hundreds of selfies on my phone, but the aughts were the final days of Polaroids and disposable cameras and photos developed by some teenage basement dweller at the drugstore and, kids, back then, photos were few and precious, even for those of us who had stacks of albums filled with dozens of photos taken over decades. I looked young when I was thirtyish, and in the only photo I have of myself during that winter, I was drunk and performing for the camera, scrunching my face up, snarling, trying my best to look like a warrior, a Viking, a Marine.

I don't know what she saw, but I felt like a swamp thing that had slithered out of the slime and wouldn't you know it, she was happy to see me regardless. She didn't cry but threw her arms open in a sort of "ta-da!" gesture— surprise! She looked older than her sixty-one years; the flight had taken its toll. It was the first time she'd flown since the attacks. The TSA was new and it seemed everyone was suspect. Especially if your skin was brown.

I could see that, and the irony was that in 2004, neither Aida nor her son were aware of their shared, occasionally debilitating anxiety. My folks grew up in an era when therapy was a last-ditch remedy for adults and children, and even though I had been sent to a shrink as a nine-year-old because I was "hyperactive," my parents were doubtful of the therapist and the expense and subtly undermined it whenever they could. For most of the twentieth century, anxiety was treated with cigarettes and alcohol and prayer, and I had prescribed myself horse doses of the first two.

I knew she was in New York City because she thought I was in trouble, and I was, in a way, but there was nothing she could do except embrace me and tell me she loved me and remind me that I had family in Texas. I didn't cry when she hugged me, but I did later, after a few swigs on the chilled bottle of emergency vodka I kept in my fridge. I couldn't believe she had come. I felt angry and helpless and I fought the tears, I ground my teeth until I tasted blood, I fell asleep half-dreaming about flinging myself in front of a Manhattan-bound N train.

We spent our first afternoon avoiding any difficult conversations. Instead, I showed her around midtown, and for a moment, she smiled. The first time

I had come home for a visit, my mom bragged to anyone who would listen that I had just gotten off the plane from New York City. She told neighbors, waiters, and sour little old ladies at church who didn't like my mom that much. (She said it was because they were racist, and I'd defend them by saying maybe it's because she talked shit about Bush every chance she got, and she said those were the same things.) Anyway, it was always "This is my son John, the New Yorker," or "My son just flew in from New York," because she believed, correctly, that New York City was the center of the universe, and in her imagination, I was riding the subway train with Leonard Bernstein and Audrey Hepburn and Duke Ellington. The blue-hairs would cluck and look at me and smirk: "Whatcha got up there ya ain't got here?" I was raised to be polite, but three months of freezing and starving in the Big Apple and calling home on pay phones and lying about how well I was doing had made me feisty. "Culture. Tolerance. Pizza," was my answer.

We ate a bagel, walked around Rockefeller Plaza, and then up to Central Park, which looks like a belligerent emerald forest that appears suddenly on the horizon as you walk up Sixth Avenue and every day that's how someone who sees the park for the first time sees it. I walked her back to her hotel, and before leaving her, I asked her to crash with me to save the money. I told her this hotel and midtown, in general, were just flypaper for out-of-towners. I suggested she check out in the morning and ask the front desk to call her a cab to my address in Astoria. I had room. Please, I said. Please.

The next morning, a stretch limo pulled in front of my apartment building in Astoria. The hotel had ripped her off and called her the most expensive car they could, and she was too embarrassed to complain once it rolled up. The concierge must have thought my mom was some wealthy Persian dowager, so they soaked her. I knew better than to call the hotel and yell at whoever was around to get yelled at. I knew better than to fight my mom's battles, even if it meant she lost them. I was infuriated, though, and I told her not to apologize. They took advantage of her! She should stand up for herself!

We hugged in the street. She was run down and overwhelmed and offered to clean my apartment. I refused her offer and lugged her suitcases up four flights of stairs. Once inside my apartment, she immediately started to sweep and wash dishes, and I stepped back when I saw it made her happy.

We stayed in Astoria that night and ate at a nice Greek restaurant, a meal of salad and broiled fish and lemon potatoes. She said the food reminded her of a Mediterranean restaurant she and Dad used to eat at back in Virginia. It was one of their favorite places to go on their date nights.

Mom asked me if I needed money the following morning, and I scoffed. But I needed money. I had thousands of dollars of credit-card debt and owed the IRS thousands more because I never paid taxes on any of the low-paying freelance blog writing I was doing on the side that paid a few bills and bought a few rounds. I'd write blog posts at fifty bucks a pop, and sometimes I'd write two or three a week while at my day job, and I never reported that income even though I had filled out W9 forms. I may or may not have known what a W9 form was at the time.

She had continued scrubbing and tidying up while I slept, and I suspect the state of my one-bedroom walk-up told her the story of a troubled young man. My apartment was furnished with knicks and knacks, mismatched chairs and broken lamps, other junk that ex-girlfriends had left behind, and a collection of milk crates I found in the trash. My stuff was dirty, old, and falling apart. And she quietly placed any drug paraphernalia she found— pipes, rolling papers, smeared mirrors—in one of my desk's broken drawers. I needed money. Yes. But I pretended I didn't, and she let me have my pride. She did, however, take a moment to peruse and praise the variety of the tattered paperbacks in my personal library.

It took forever to get from Astoria to Williamsburg on the subway, especially with my mom in tow. But she was in awe of the speeding trains and all the different kinds of people and the noise. She had always been the fearless one in the family, who'd zip up our creaky ladder to the roof to clean the gutters or drive in a treacherous blizzard to pick up tortillas at the good grocery store because you can't have taquitos without them. She had a round scar on the back of her hand that she claimed she gave herself trying to burn off a gang tattoo with a car's cigarette lighter. Was it true? I have no idea. She always had stories about the old days in El Paso. But she was tough, and she taught me what she knew. When I was being bullied in third grade, for instance, she told me what to do: kick my tormentor in the testicles, like a football player punting a pigskin. This was what she was taught by her dad. You hit back, hard, or you'll get hit again and again. So it was difficult to watch her walk carefully, cautiously, as if she was made out of delicate porcelain.

I made it a point to stop by a taqueria to show my mom that our people were doing well in the big city. In the late '90s, New York's Latino population was almost exclusively a mix of Puerto Ricans and Dominicans, with a smattering of immigrants from Cuba and a bunch of Central American countries. But Mexicans were new to the scene, hopefuls who had made the long trek from Puebla and Oaxaca to Queens and parts of Brooklyn. I like to think I was part of this exodus north, but the large Mexican family that lived above me in the cramped house I was renting in 1996, my first apartment in the city, did not consider me one of them and saw me for who I was, a white boy with parents who could fly him home if they had to. I moved through the world as a white man, judged by non-whites and whites for different reasons. To the family upstairs, I was not to be trusted, but to the publishing world, I was, at best, a C+ student who lived out-of-state in Queens.

After a short, friendly conversation in Spanish with the taqueria owners, she told me they were from Arizona and the tacos were "so-so."

* * *

The entrance to The Brick is unassuming, a few steps from the corner of Metropolitan Avenue and Lorimer Street. It's easy to miss. It looks like a chop shop, but once you step in it's Alice through the garage door and, instead of cars and tools and the smell of gasoline, it's a modest theater full of actors and their natural byproduct, the psychic stuff they leave behind that landlords and developers covet—for a short amount of time, that is—and that substance is what legendary Broadway dance god and human superfund site Bob Fosse called the old "razzle dazzle."

If you charge artists inexpensive rents, they'll create galleries out of shuttered storefronts, and turn garages into small theaters and open quirky coffee shops that attract the young and the wild and those who pay good money to be in the company of both the young and the wild. The art brings the hip bars and those who want to party, and before you know it, the suits and the squares and the trust-fund spawn follow because they're all born followers. By that point, rents have been jacked, the artists have been flushed out, and the cycle begins anew in the corner of some unloved and neglected urban neighborhood.

But during the lifespan of a scrappy arts space on the wrong side of the tracks, the newcomers and the families who call that part of town home gently coexist, and the local businesses benefit from a modest boost from those artists buying cheap beer from corner stores and slices from the pizza place that's been there forever. The relationship only becomes strained once the party princesses start puking after hours and then, of course, when your grandmother's apartment becomes too expensive to live in.

The Brick, as an institution, did not pursue unnecessary controversy. It didn't hurt that Robert was a centaur—a half-lawyer, half–performance artist who would act naked in a one-man *King Lear* if Michael asked. He made sure that The Brick was a good neighbor for legal reasons and because of good ol' fashioned Texas manners. He knew New York City preferred its artists to be seen and not heard, like Victorian children. Robert and Michael kept their word to the landlords too. No one ever bothered the old guys at the corner bar, and those coots never checked out what the freaks were up to in the garage.

If my mother suspected that I was spending my days eating frozen pizzas and drinking the kind of vodka that could clean surgical scalpels, she didn't say anything to me. She just quietly bagged the pizza boxes and bottles and kept sweeping and cleaning. But I could see her relief when the cast of *In a Strange Room* greeted her warmly, with smiles and hugs. Michael was especially welcoming and made it a point to tell her how thrilled he was to work with me again. He offered to escort my mom into The Box, but she said she'd watch from outside and swore she would not make a sound. I remember Michael invited her to cheer or boo, to make a ruckus if she wanted. She surprised me, too, by telling Michael she had read *As I Lay Dying* many years ago and preferred his novel *Sanctuary*, and the two shared a brief conversation about those books. I had never read *Sanctuary* either, but I didn't let on.

As the rehearsal began, Ivanna and Hope sat beside her and pulled out their knitting, which they did during the long rehearsals when they weren't on stage. She was charmed by the wholesomeness of their long scarves. I went outside to take a call, but I smoked a cigarette instead. Instead of quitting smoking, she and I just hid our habits from each other, knowing full well that tobacco killed him. When I entered, the rehearsal was in full swing, a crowd of grown-ups shouting and stomping and playing an intense game of make-believe. I forget what scene they were rehearsing, but my mom was a giving audience member, laughing at every elongated vowel.

I introduced her during a break to Mikki and Robert, and I asked her if she wanted to stay or go, and she insisted we stay. Your friends, she said, they're so sweet. Then, with a hint of surprise in her voice: and they like you!

After the rehearsal, I surprised her with two tickets to composer Alan Menken and lyricist Howard Ashman's shlock-camp masterpiece *Little Shop of Horrors* on Broadway, which I bought using a brand-new credit card I was sent by the same bank that was harassing me for my inconsistent payments. *Little Shop of Horrors* was a smash Off-Broadway hit that had been turned into a hit 1986 movie directed by Frank Oz and starring my best friend Rick Moranis, Steve Martin, and the original Audrey, Ellen Greene. But it had never made it to the Great White Way until 2003.

(One of the main differences between Hollywood's *Little Shop of Horrors* and Off-Broadway's was the ending. The original musical ends with the alien plant eating everyone, including Seymour and Audrey. The final song, "Finale Ultimo (Don't Feed the Plant)," warns the audience to be careful what they wish for. It's performed by Audrey and his Earth-devouring offspring, played by his many victims. The big-budget Broadway production, which starred Hunter Foster, who had made a name starring on Broadway in *Urinetown*, the Fringe's biggest hit, embraced the bleaker finale.)

The last play we had seen together had been in Austin before I evacuated Texas, a one-man show about Jack Kerouac that she saw advertised in the newspaper and bought tickets for. She knew I was a fan of the famous beat writer, a rebel and a fuck-up who drank himself to death at the ancient age of 47. I read his sloppy memoirs like *On the Road* and *The Dharma Bums*, exhausting confessions fueled by uppers about men, real men, completely confused and riled up by their big, stupid feelings. I was drawn to alcoholics, and it is funny that I was unable to see why. All I knew was that Kerouac was in pain and was able to transform that pain into words, like some kind of alchemist tramp, and he was celebrated for it.

The actor playing Kerouac agreed with me, mostly. He was probably five years older than me, a graduate of UT, and the space was a room above a coffeehouse downtown. We were one of five or so audience members, and his show was fairly zippy. His Kerouac was a droning street tough spouting poetry, and it ended with him sticking his thumb out to hitchhike and . . . blackout.

The show had bored my mom, but it was welcome evidence that my master plan would, first, require that I, too, self-produce plays that no one would see and that would put me in debt. Then, after that, Broadway. *Little Shop of Horrors* was big and bright, and watching it with my mom felt like a pair of warm socks plucked fresh from the dryer.

This was our last night together. I treated us to a midnight snack at a diner by my house: scrambled eggs, toast, and soup. She couldn't stop talking about the knitting and Michael, and she finally told me my apartment was very messy and I shouldn't let it get that messy. What if I had friends over? she said.

During a pause, as I scraped butter over toast and she slurped chicken and rice from her spoon, I asked her if she still thought about him every day and she said "Yes," quietly, and then asked me the same thing. Do you think about him? "Yes," I lied. All it took was a snort, a chug, a pill to forget about him, sometimes for a night. Easy. On the walk back to my apartment, she told me he'd be proud of me, and I was incredulous. Why? I was barely making ends meet; it's not like doing theatre in Brooklyn was making me any money; I was single. Seriously: why would he be proud? Because, she said, you're trying. I thought about that for a moment. Then I asked her if she was proud of me, and she responded: I have always had faith in you.

The next morning I called a cab and made sure that Aida got in it and the driver knew to take her to LaGuardia. She kissed me on the cheek and the forehead, and as she drove away, I couldn't shake the feeling that would be the last time I would ever see her again.

* * *

Later that week, Yvonne would write me an email out of the blue. She was checking in on me. The email was the basics: Hello, how are you, I'm happy. Short and sweet. I don't know why I didn't respond. It was late, and I was tired, but the most plausible reason I didn't email her back because it didn't matter how I was, and I didn't care that she was okay in Vancouver with her optimistic boyfriend and that they probably hiked and drank IPAs and lived in a huge, beautiful, cheap apartment with a view of a huge, beautiful mountain.

It had been years. I hadn't talked to her since before 9/11, and did she call me after 9/11? Maybe? I'm not sure? I don't remember because I was busy doing stuff I can't quite remember, especially for the first two months after that nightmare. She wasn't here, and she hadn't emailed me, and I hadn't emailed or called her either, to be perfectly fair.

But even if I wanted to email her back—let's say, for the sake of argument—I don't know what I'd tell her. "Dear Yvonne, I am happy you are happy. That must be nice. What's it like? As for me: I would like to die as quickly and painlessly as possible, but I'm chickenshit, so please send some encouragement. Give my best to what's-his-name! Love, John. P.S. How much are cigarettes in Canada because in NYC, they're almost nine bucks because Mayor Bloomberg is a fascist."

I settled on forgetting she ever emailed me. I like to think there's an alternate reality in the multiverse where a version of you is living the life you dreamed of and getting everything you ever wanted, and in that reality, Yvonne and I are co–artistic directors of a fabulously well-funded theater where I write plays and act in them, and we both teach, and we both have

the exact same streak of silver in our hair. The Yvonne and me of this perfect world spend our days nurturing young artists and our nights rehearsing,
and on the weekends, we brunch with each other's spouses, who are both
accomplished people who love their work and their families, and on Saturday
nights, I go to the movies to see big, dumb, loud superhero movies.

But this did not happen. She moved away, and I stayed.

* * *

I worked for an editor in the late '90s who was fond of military sayings
like this one from General Patton: "Never tell people how to do things. Tell
them what to do, and they will surprise you with their ingenuity." He'd say
that before telling me exactly how to do my job. He was also fond of "No
plan survives contact with the enemy," a pithy morsel written by nineteenth-
century Prussian field marshal Helmuth von Moltke in an 1871 essay about
military strategy.

"No plan survives contact with the enemy, John," he'd growl, and he
was talking about the editorial calendar. He was an old shoe who thought
reviewing office printers was a calling and the internet was a fad like disco
music. I ran into him a few months after 9/11 on the Upper West Side; I was
running to a bar, and he was running to an old record shop on 72nd, and
we chatted on a street corner. We exchanged pleasantries, and he told me the
next 100 years would be a nightmare, just shootings and wars, poverty and
environmental damage, and most of us would be trapped inside, staring at
screens and screaming.

Helmuth von Moltke's wisdom can be applied to the theatre. The same
elements required to launch an attack are those needed for opening a play:
vision, planning, practice, and execution. And what does it take to pre-
vail? Against long odds? Adaptability. Perseverance. When the battle goes

pear-shaped, improvise. There's a reason the military calls any area where armed conflict is happening a "theater of war."

The week before the first show is stressful, but that is to be expected. That is just the way it is. One of the most enduring rules of theatre is the "dress rehearsal" rule, which states that a terrible dress rehearsal means an incredible opening night. This rule is as important and foundational to theatre kids as Newton's laws of motion are to physicists. This is theatre kids 101.

It's no guarantee. I know from experience it's possible to have a bad dress rehearsal and an even worse opening night. But it is a comforting lie, especially when the lights aren't working and the sound cues can't be heard. Then it becomes a matter of faith: "The dress rehearsal is a disaster, but everything will be okay in a few nights." The theatre runs on two primary fuels: adrenaline and faith, with caffeine and nicotine serving as emergency alternatives if the first two run out.

The dress rehearsal for *In a Strange Room* was intense and occasionally bumpy, but it went relatively smoothly, to the point that it made the cast and crew suspicious.

After giving us his extensive notes and releasing us for the night, Michael gave us the best pep talk he could, a short speech where he nervously told us what an excellent job we had done and how grateful he was for our work. Then he told us to break a leg, and that was that.

What made Michael a good director wasn't necessarily his artistic vision, which was focused, creative, and ambitious. The truth is, *In a Strange Room* had potential, and Michael needed what any production with potential needs to grow, and that's time and money, and I've never known what it's like to have either. One thing Mr. Boyd taught me during rehearsals for a night of student-directed one-acts was that directors leap first. That's the deal, he told me. Michael was always willing to accept those terms.

So we all went home after dress rehearsal feeling relatively positive about *In a Strange Room*, Brooklyn's only experimental literary happening performed entirely in a really big wooden box.

Meanwhile, the approaching show opening unlocked in me a long-dormant and intense confidence in good-luck charms. It's one of the things actors and athletes have in common, a belief that the universe can be influenced by wishing on stars and clutching rabbit's feet. I should add that drunks are superstitious too.

Despite my boozing and inability to memorize my lines, I developed a stage fright that I remedied by sneaking the plastic statue of the Virgin Mary with the screw-top crown into my little corner of the dressing room. I started doing this during tech week. I would take it backstage in my pants and hide it underneath my clothes, but not before holding it in my hands like it had magic properties. And if I didn't squeeze the Virgin Mary and say a little prayer before my first scene, I was convinced I'd spontaneously combust. This ritual was a secret between me and the mother of Jesus Christ, and only the two of us.

* * *

There were opening-night jitters, which are the best kind of jitters, if you ask me. There are few jitters to compare to the very first performance of a live play after months of rehearsal. The first that come to mind are Christmas Eve and, maybe, standing in line to ride a big loop-de-loop roller coaster at an amusement park. Waiting for both is exquisite. Waiting for a pizza to be delivered after a long day of yard work is torture, but it's worth it.

The director's job is over the moment the final dress rehearsal ends. From that point on, once the audience is let in, every play or musical or live event belongs to the stage manager. Stage managers exist outside the drama of theatre productions; they're like seraphim, floating above it all, issuing commands from the firmament. But seraphim who wear nothing but black.

In a Strange Room had a stage manager. She was a friend of Ivanna. The show probably couldn't have happened without her calling the shots from the claustrophobic tech booth, which was crammed with light boards and electronics and a small fan that tried its best to cool whoever was stuck up there, flipping switches and pushing buttons. And while the stage manager made sure all 10,000 lighting, sound, and fog machine cues were on time (and they were, 96.9 percent of the time), Michael sat in The Box with the audience, smiling, admiring his own handiwork.

The stage manager is not part of the cast. Not exactly. They are exacting and detail-oriented, and many, though not all, can drink incredible amounts of beer. A stage manager is a frame of mind, a priesthood, a gender. They love actors and directors, and actors and directors are constantly breaking their hearts.

Our stage manager was friendly and would take photos of the cast. We chatted often. But she never got too close. Like a secret service agent, she had a job. Responsibilities I could never understand, that I could never bear.

The second time I truly knew that *In a Strange Room* was real, that actual people were buying tickets to sit down and watch it, was when the stage manager first said: five minutes 'til curtain! That's when the adrenaline starts to surge like warm water through a garden hose.

You find your place backstage and everyone, actors and audience members, floats in the darkness and silence, for a moment. In the void, there's a cough as the crowd nervously, excitedly waits for the lights to snap to life, and they do, and the play begins.

It is every actor's choice whether or not they step into the spotlight. It is a leap of faith every single time. The theatre is full of folk tales of actors who got cold feet and ran or slept through curtain. I could have bailed. There was no one stopping me from just not showing up—and the show would have gone on. I would have disappointed the cast, but theatre kids are famously resourceful, and I'm sure someone would have jumped in and recited my lines because everyone had memorized my lines except for me.

That's what's exciting about the theatre. It lives like Frankenstein's monster, and like his sensitive, temperamental, unloved creation, the theatre is unpredictable and charged. The taste of that electricity is at its most pungent on opening night. You can feel it in your teeth. You're alive. There is only you and them and Dionysus. You're alive, and you won't always be. One day you'll be a skull with spiders in your eye sockets, so step into the light while you can.

I was as shocked as anyone that first night that we managed to finish the entire play with a bare minimum of fuck-ups. The curtain call in The Box was tight; we formed a ring inside and faced the audience, standing in their laps and politely bowing, for there was only room for a polite bow, which is my favorite bow style. It's a bow that says, "I'm exhausted, thank you, I did it all for you and you."

There are three basic kinds of theatre bows. The most popular looks like you're slowly bending over and touching your toes and then rising again and smiling at the crowd. The next version is a variation, where you hold the hand of the actor next to you, and you bend over together, like a family, a tight-knit, incestuous family that will never see each other again after the show closes.

I find those bows difficult to perform, but I like to think I'm a master of the third bow, and all casts should be legally compelled to nod their head toward the applause simply, and maybe smirk a little, maybe exhale, before quickly, nimbly, fucking off stage.

There are a few variations that I begrudgingly approve of: It is fine to clasp your hands together to your heart. Not too much, though. And if the spirit moves you, I approve of one instance of applauding for the audience who are applauding for you. Again: don't milk it. I know we do it for the applause, but begging isn't dignified.

There is nothing like getting paid to play for a living, but being praised by strangers because of your powers of make-believe is a surprisingly satisfying consolation prize. An actor's most important performance is how to ask for and receive acclaim.

* * *

One show down. Fifteen to go.

Nothing extinguishes human energy faster than performing for three people, which is not something any of us had planned on, even though The Box could only hold a dozen plus one audience member. No one planned for a sold-out house, but c'mon. And to make matters worse, you'd think three people would fill up the snug set, but they just made it feel emptier and knew it. It turns out that having to watch thirteen actors stampede and emote for four hours is both emotionally and physically exhausting, and one of the three bailed at intermission.

One of my favorite theatre kid cliches is "the show must go on," a well-intentioned rallying cry when the chips are down that has been co-opted by bosses everywhere who don't want to pay overtime. Few mantras describe the theatre kid vibe as efficiently as the "show must go on," which is a clarion call to suffer and smile, to push through the pain even if the pain is telling you to stop because you're hurting yourself. A theatre kid is a tempest of glitter and jazz hands who must spin, no matter what. Sprained ankle? Spin! Stomach bug? Try not to barf, but spin! A small house of bored people who don't want to see live theatre? Spin, spin, spin! The show must go on!

The show must go on, which means you live in the moment and act like your ass is on fire. You show whoever bought a ticket a good time, you perspire for their pleasure, and you graciously receive their applause, even if it's one pair of clammy hands slapping together. And afterward, you complain with the rest of the family, but only once the curtains have lowered, and the audience has left the theater.

There are few professionals more professional than unpaid actors working on a production they believe in, and most of the cast believed in *In a Strange Room,* from its grumpy leading man who grew distant during tech week only to summon forth a mumbling, calculating demon bumpkin every night, to Alyssa and Chime's captivating sexy horse dance. All the actors showed up inspired, ready to work, and committed actors can save any production, no matter how troubled. Those who had lost confidence in Michael's direction still had faith in their abilities. Even Jeff and the knee-high terror finally made peace, and they both conducted themselves with dedication and aplomb during the run.

Eventually, I established a pattern. I'd show up right at call, an hour before lights-up. I was usually the last to stroll in, and by that point, the entire cast would be getting ready for the night's performance: not just warming up but communing with Dionysus, the god who loves to kiss strangers on the dance floor. He lives in every theater and church and watches over fools. When an actor prays, it is Dionysus who listens, drunk.

This sacred time is when actors meditate, get the blood flowing, and find the inner strength to stand in front of a crowd and say something truly ridiculous, which can be summed up thusly: "Hello, I am now a different person." You aren't, but the audience goes ahead and agrees anyway and that's *[*jazz hands*]* theatre.

While the cast prepares, the director despairs.

The temperament of theatre directors is best visualized as a spectrum with fascist at one end and flibbertigibbet at the other. Michael was center-flibbertigibbet. He was always juggling one or two hatchets when I'd show up, hissing commands to the stage manager or the volunteers manning the box office.

He looked skinny and haggard, but I knew he was at his happiest during the hectic run-up to the show, and he seemed to be the only person who was never discouraged by the small-to-nonexistent audiences who were showing up or not showing up, depending on the night. It turns out the core demographic for *In a Strange* Room—the audience who most wanted to watch staged Faulkner adaptations—was mostly just Michael, who made a meal out of every minute of every performance, God bless him. He was broke, insignificant, and happy for four hours every night. Four hours.

The most beautiful words in the entire theatre lexicon are "ninety minutes, no intermission." I'm not dismissing the thrills of a well-timed intermission. There are intermissions that are rescue ladders and intermissions that give you a chance to catch your breath, empty your bladder, and settle back into your seat, ready for more. From the cast's point of view, an intermission is the halfway mark, a smoke break, and the last lap before drinks and snacks around the corner.

I prefer my theatre zippy, no midshow speed bump, but there's a time and place for a play that bends space and time that requires a breather. I have sat through three-hour-long productions of *Henry V* and *Hamlet* and been absorbed by the Bard's ancient words and the actors' inventive interpretations of those words and the clever director's stylish stagings. I have also had my mind melted by plays that went on and on and on, blue-collar sob stories and classics written during historical periods when audiences had two entertainment options: watch endless plays about unhappy landowners or read the same story in a book by candlelight.

I have only ever walked out on a show during an intermission two times in my life, and they were both Broadway shows, one a dismal Disney musical and the other a Tennessee Williams revival that was so faithful to the suffering playwright's famous excesses that I started to wonder if he was, in fact, the worst dramatist of all time.

I don't know how many audience members fled The Box the moment they were allowed out during intermission. I spent those fifteen minutes smoking across the street or calling my drug dealer on my cell phone. I spent one intermission snorting bumps of coke off a key next to a nearby dumpster, powdered courage.

The second half of *In a Strange Room* was more action-packed and demented, even though you had to be led back into The Box like cattle. I knew the show was interminable but every night I was transfixed at least once by one of my fellow cast members' choices, an unexpected demon laugh or a sudden, anguished grunt. I didn't want to be there, but I did, which was an honest reflection of my mental health.

A couple of critics showed up, and very few members of the Off-Off-Broadway community made the trek to Williamsburg, which stung Michael, who loyally sought out the work of other experimental theatre artists. This annoyed me because I knew plenty of those dipshits with their noses in the air and their glowing *Village Voice* reviews and their talent and determination and dedication. I wanted to fight them, but I also knew what they knew: The Brick was a small, deeply uncool theater run by and for nerds.

Then, one night, acclaimed American sculptor Richard Serra sat in The Box. The sixty-six-year-old was the uncle of Chime, who played Jewel, the gruff, gravel-mouthed Bundren with a hard-on for his horse. I did not know who Serra was when I was told that one of the greatest living artists was coming to see the show, a towering figure whose gigantic abstract works had inspired awe all around the globe. "Have you ever seen a Serra?" I was asked repeatedly, and by the third or fourth time, I lied. "Epic," I'd say, and the person asking would nod.

Serra was not only the most famous person to see *In a Strange Room*, out of the dozens who would buy a ticket, but he was the most famous person to have come to The Brick, topped only later by a unique twosome: the playwright and former Czech republic president Vaclav Havel and former Secretary of State Madeleine Albright, who was his date to a 2006 festival The Brick produced honoring Havel's revolutionary plays.

I had never seen a famous artist, and so during one of the long periods during this show when I wasn't performing, I snuck a peek at Serra through the slots of The Box and saw the melting face of a man bored and annoyed. He was thoroughly unimpressed with his nephew's play, and if he could have walked out, I think he would, but, thankfully, he was pinned to his seat by the fury of actors stomping and whooping, possessed by the ghost of William Faulkner.

I didn't blame him. I had become bored with the Bundrens and with the theatre, which I started to resent because the theatre represented time I could have spent at a bar, or a strip club, or anywhere else. After each show, Michael would make it a point to offer me sincere encouragement, but my heart wasn't there.

The theatre required a mindfulness that had begun to frustrate me. Why would anyone want to be in the present? In the moment? When I can exist in various futures where I am successful and happy and far beyond the reach of consequences?

There were a few cast members who lobbied Michael immediately after opening, a few final attempts to convince him this or that should change and he listened, intently, to their insecurities and disloyalties and then went about his business. The show would not change.

But after the first weekend, *In a Strange Room* settled into a fairly competent groove. There's an old chestnut about there being no small parts, just small actors, and I think that can apply to audiences too.

I felt disconnected from Michael and Robert and Ivanna, from all of them, save for Mikki, who looked me in the eyes, and I worried about what would happen if she saw the real me, the me that couldn't handle the feelings, any of the feelings, the tears, the laughter, the me that preferred to look up at the world from the bottom of an ocean of booze. It's safe down there, in the dark. But cold.

* * *

Mikki and I first kissed in the snow. A few days before, I had worked up the nerve to pass her a hand-written note, like the kinds I'd sneak Julie during work, and the note was a message asking her out. On the folded piece of paper, I had scrawled "Will you go out with me?" as if I were a sixth grader and there was a "Yes" box and a "No" box. During rehearsal, as Anse and the boys thundered and bickered, she checked the "Yes" box and quietly slid it back to me.

She smiled at me, and I smiled back. During the break, we sheepishly made a low-stakes plan to have a coffee before the start of Saturday's rehearsal, the last weekend before opening night. It was flurrying on the way to the coffee shop, and during our date, the snow started to come down in great white waves.

The conversation was gentle. Mikki had a quality that I was unaware that a person could have, a stillness and a quiet counterbalanced by a knack for filling a room with light and warmth. Her Dewey Dell had slowly evolved during rehearsal into a simultaneously vulnerable and determined young woman, and I like to think Mikki mined her own character for Dewey. I watched her every night in awe and felt mismatched during our hilariously sinister scene.

I was completely honest with her, which felt so liberating. I was completely honest, except I didn't tell her about my credit card debt, and slowly ballooning cocaine budget, and my drinking and crying, and I definitely didn't tell her about Julie or, really, *Maxim*, which, objectively, was gross to a great many very smart and sensitive people. That was a solid foundation for a relationship, right? Complete and total and selective truth.

It never occurred to me that my loneliness and self-hatred didn't make me special, that countless human beings just like me would rather claw the skin off their faces than turn to the people they love the most and admit they'd be lost without them.

There were so many of us, unhappy, and scared. You cannot hide and love others. You have to allow yourself to be seen, and be vulnerable. You have to unclench your fist and open your hand, and heart. I knew these things, and the more time I spent with Mikki, the more I thought "I can do this." I could love and be loved.

Mikki and I had more than a few things in common. We both moved to the Big City because we had Master Plans, and hers were radically upended by the horrors of September 11, 2001. She had been in the financial district that day temping, and I could tell she was still wrestling with that trauma. I watched the attacks on TV from the Flatiron District, a two-and-a-half-mile walk north from where the city was burning. I remember walking up an empty Sixth Avenue as F-16 fighters screamed overhead. I had my first shot of bourbon around eleven in the morning, and I watched the smoke from the roof of my apartment in Astoria, and I remember smelling and tasting the ash, a mix of steel and bones. But Mikki had fought back from a dark place and was helping others who had directly suffered while acting in various experimental shows all around the city. She asked me about myself, too, and I did my level best not just to grunt or give her one-word answers. I told her about my dad and his cancer, and I tried to act like I was over. I shrugged and said, "Whaddya do?" This was a rhetorical question because here's what you do: You press a pillow over your pain and whisper "shhh, shhhh" while you smother it until it stops fighting you back, and then you relax until it returns, bigger, sharper, meaner. She didn't press me for details, she just listened, and I think I fell in love with her right there.

I had meant to be succinct and mysterious, but before I knew it, I was telling her about some of my favorite things, like a singing nun, including my favorite Shakespeare play (*King Lear*), my favorite band (The Pixies), and my favorite Greek restaurant in Queens (Elias Corner). I did not tell her I wanted to have a beer right then and there, which I chalked up to progress. I was growing! I was having coffee with an attractive, intelligent, sensitive woman who wasn't married to someone who wanted to maim me. She was, in fact, single and funny and interested in me. She listened intently. We were harmonizing, sober and silly.

It's not like she was a teetotaler, but she was a person who was in a constant, honest conversation with herself about her wants and fears, and I could tell that inner debate was exhausting, but it's how she survived her traumas. To her, drinking was fun. I had seen Mikki drink before, which she did with style. She was a Scotch drinker and would sip her booze with a half smirk. I watched her after rehearsal once from afar, and I blushed when she met my eyes. I blushed and didn't order another drink and left so I could go to another bar, far away, a bar where I could hide and debase myself.

I did not know at that point in my life that the vast majority of people have one or two drinks a week, sometimes more, sometimes they get drunk on their birthday or on New Year's Eve, and every so often things will get out of hand, and they'll need to stop drinking for awhile, and they do.

And then there are people like me, and I did not fully understand people like me at all.

We walked to rehearsal down the street in the snow. The city was quiet and slow, and we walked carefully, our feet crunch-crunching as snowflakes decorated our hair. I briefly worried about what would happen when she saw me drunk, which was inevitable, as much as I wanted to think I could control myself. I couldn't. But that worry disappeared when we stopped walking and looked at each other and kissed. This wouldn't be some show romance, I thought to myself. This would last.

I don't believe in telepathy, clairvoyance, or supernatural powers. I grew up reading *X-Men* comic books, all about outcasts who could shoot lasers out of their eyes and read minds.

My mom claimed her grandmother, my great-grandmother, was a shaman over in Mexico and that she could ward off the evil eye, but I correctly dismissed those tales as hocus-pocus.

I'm open to being wrong. I want to live in a world where a sacred few can perform miracles, like having a sixth sense, or flying. And Mikki seemed like an ideal candidate for such gifts. She saw me and didn't wince. Our gazes would meet while warming up preshow, and I wouldn't look away. Mikki would ask me if I was okay, and I'd say yes, and I wasn't. And she knew it. She could sense it. During the performance, we would hold hands in the dark until it was her cue or mine.

* * *

I don't think we ever sold out a house. At most, ten audience members sat in that box and watched a retelling of a story that had little to do with the first few years of the twenty-first century. Faulkner was writing about the rural South during the start of the Great Depression, when you could still find a few old-timers who fought for the Confederacy, telling stories about the lost cause to their grandchildren.

If you squinted during 1930, you could see, in the distance, the years of suffocating poverty that was coming and the war, but Faulkner's Bundrens weren't thinking about the future. They had their minds on surviving another day in a forgotten county in a bankrupt state that was once part of a failed nation. They did what they had to to get by, get ahead, and get a new set of teeth. The United States is a young country that has boomed, collapsed, and boomed again, and all the while, there is a country inside the country populated by people born with nothing or born with a boot on their neck.

The *As I Lay Dying* of 2004 would have starred the Bundrens, a family deep in hock, living in a McMansion in some bleak suburb outside a struggling mid-size city, all of them zonked out on antidepressants and cable news and internet porn. When it came time to spread Addie's ashes, Anse, the boys, and Dewey Dell would pile into their SUV and bicker the whole way while listening to Rush Limbaugh. I pitched Michael this idea during one of our walks during the first few weeks of rehearsal, and while I laughed at it, I could tell it repulsed him. He wasn't trying to comment on modern America or, frankly, the America of the late 1920s. To him, *As I Lay Dying* was a timeless story about a fucked-up family, and it's timeless specifically because all families are fucked-up. The entirety of life is fucked-up, from crib to coffin; every king and every slave thinks "That's it?" as they take their last breath.

It's not that Michael wasn't political. He had an enormous appetite for news and had plenty of opinions about the country. He openly opposed the war. We spent one afternoon futzing around the space, sweeping and tidying up, talking about Saddam's "rape rooms," one of a half dozen or so scary stories the Bush administration was circulating to drum up support for the war. That specific story was horrifying and, in my opinion, a little too horrifying to be true.

I think about the phone call I had with my dad right after the terrorist attacks. Right before we got off the phone, after saying "I love you" to each other, he said, "Don't worry, Son." What he said next was meant to give me courage. We were both so scared. He said America would bomb those bastards, we'd get back at whoever was responsible for killing all those people, and that felt good to hear. It made me feel strong, and I repeated, "We'll bomb those bastards" because it kept me from crying. The Bush administration exploited those feelings with disturbing confidence and sophistication. Then they liberally salted revenge with existential terror and suggested Saddam was, suddenly, a nuclear power.

Michael and I agreed that some dictators deserve obliteration, but rushing to war against a country that may or may not have been responsible for the 9/11 attacks was probably an extremely bad idea. The country wanted blood, and if you weren't screaming for scalps, you were ignored or mocked, or steamrolled by politicians and the press, and the vast majority of Americans.

Despite the chaos, however, Michael stayed focused on Faulkner's taxidermy collection of spiritually lost yokels. The war was outside The Box. Inside The Box, the human condition.

But that's me projecting again. I have no idea what Michael was trying to say with his show, if he was trying to say anything. Michael didn't aspire to Brecht; his theatre wasn't directly political. I think I've always admired Brecht for thinking that art changes minds and hearts and society, but Michael was too much of a devotee of Foreman to comment on socio-economic issues. There was no larger cultural subtext. No direct social critique. Michael was not a postmodernist.

No, his *As I Lay Dying* was a Schechner-esque happening, a giant, reckless, seemingly improvised but methodically composed matrix, and inside that matrix, you would have no choice but to let waves of sound and light, smoke and words crash over you until you surrendered, and sipped, and drowned and floated.

And yet. . . .

In a Strange Room ends with Anse Bundren triumphant, with a new set of teeth stuffed in his mouth bought with money he stole from his daughter and a brand-new wife by his side, a woman who sold him the shovels used to bury Addie. He introduces her to the family: "Meet Mrs. Bundren." It is a rude final note before an abrupt, equally rude blackout.

Michael succeeded, in those last few seconds, to transmute his wooden box into another thing, an otherwordly thing, a room in hell crowded with lost souls ruined by grief and selfishness. The first time I watched this final tableau—Anse grinning, his family aghast—from outside The Box, I gasped. And each subsequent time I felt an uneasiness in my guts. I was condemned to the darkness with the Bundrens. And when the lights came back up, I took my bows.

The critics who showed up didn't like the play. David didn't review it because it would have been a gross conflict of interest, and the critic he sent was dismissive of Michael's massive achievement. Some houses were more supportive than others; one night, the audience was a smattering of living mannequins and Alexis, an actor and writer from Staten Island who was part Italian-American grandma and part punk-band lead singer. She was one of those actors who you could point at and shout "act" and they would, without trying hard at all, and you wouldn't be able to keep your eyes off of her. The other paying customers looked shell-shocked the whole time but Alexis was engaged, laughing and gasping with the power of ten ticket buyers. There was one night when a pair of tourists showed up looking for a cultural adventure and found *In a Strange Room* listed in the very back of that week's issue of *Time Out New York*. They left during intermission. I suggested to Michael we should not have an intermission and just drive through all four hours like a trucker on meth.

In a Strange Room—and The Brick—were never going to make back their money. Never. The whole production was a hard sell, to say the least. Most audiences want to be comfortable. They don't want to sit in a box for hours, staring up at actors performing, literally, in their faces. They don't want to suffer for their art. Most audiences want to laugh or cry or sing, maybe all three, maybe nap a little, maybe nod along to a political message, and they want to do this from the safety of their seat. The show was a box-office flop, which surprised no one.

And it ended its run as a critical failure too. But after the cast took their final bows, Michael couldn't have seemed happier.

The show had moments, beautiful and disturbing moments, and it was also messy, boring, pretentious, but by God, it was all those things, boldly. I don't know if the show was good, on the whole. I still don't have any real perspective. I don't think I would have gone to see *In a Strange Room* if I didn't know anyone in it. It just wouldn't have sounded like something I'd want to spend money on. But I don't know that for sure. A few years later, in 2006, the avant-garde troupe Elevator Repair Service put on an eight-hour-long production of F. Scott Fitzgerald's *The Great Gatsby* called *Gatz*, where a cast of thirteen acted out and read every single word of that novel to critical acclaim. It was the downtown theatre event of the year, an alleged masterpiece, complete with a dinner break. I remember David asking me over an email if I had any interest in seeing it and I didn't respond because it sounded like hell. I did wonder why that literary endurance test was celebrated, and Michael's was not.

That's the thing about being an alcoholic: you can never have too many resentments.

* * *

The closing-night cast party for *In a Strange Room* took place at The Brick, which became a sort of social club after hours. At that time of night, there were increasing numbers of partygoers staggering past the theater toward Union Pool who were oblivious to what was going on in the garage, although every so often, a couple of drunk women would walk in, thinking this space was some hip new speakeasy, only to find a theater filled with dorks drinking wine out of mugs and red Solo cups.

The final show was the best it had ever been, a well-oiled machine powered by electricity and blood and words, and Robert's laughter, the laughter of a broken man, hung in the rafters until after the six or so audience members slowly, carefully, stepped out of The Box and down the narrow stairs, carefully, their feet wobbling a little, their legs cramped and lower backs sore.

That night's house included some family and friends who hung out a bit as Michael and the stage manager cleaned up the space. Mikki and I were careful to hide our budding romance even though everyone knew. But there was an unspoken wariness between us, a fear of moving too fast or rashly. Her last relationship had deflated, so she wasn't in a rush. I was swerving like a drunk driver between telling her I loved her and calling Julie. Whenever Mikki caught my eye, she'd smile slyly because we had a secret, and I was already sick with secrets.

There is no organizing a closing-night cast party; they sprout. Within an hour of the last performance of *In a Strange Room* ever, bottles of wine and bags of chips magically appeared, as had a rogue's gallery of performance artists, dancers, actors, electronic music composers, and clowns, and I don't mean birthday clowns, I mean people who studied clowning in Europe and their clowns were terrifying and sexual. Their laughter was the shriek of someone being held down and tickled.

The party did not rage because The Brick was not built by ragers. It was built by friends with patience and a talent for paperwork. Robert and Michael were like eccentric uncles who were cheerful and supportive and just . . . nice. Nice. Disturbingly nice. That's the only word for it, and it sounds so trite. I wish I had a talent for that virtue—for niceness—which is frequently maligned unfairly. The world desperately needs nice people. It would be intolerable without them, even the corny, insufferable ones. Niceness is confused with weakness but that's not true. Kindness is compassion with a thick hide, it is strength and hope and tenderness, no matter what. Nice people are disciplined; they actively choose kindness, at first, even if the situation may, ultimately, require a different tack. Robert and Michael were always nice to me. They chose to be, even when I was cruel or dismissive or shit-faced.

The Brick was built to shelter and embrace. The original mission wasn't quite so lofty. Robert and Michael wanted a place where they could feature their work, and one day, an entire parade of vaudevillians showed up at their door, and their career as impresarios began. A few months after they opened, I staged a play there about dueling soccer moms who make pacts with the devil. The lighting system wasn't complete, and there weren't any risers or chairs, but I put on a play they produced. It was fun, and absolutely no one came to see it, no matter how much I begged coworkers and drinking buddies to take the L train to Brooklyn. That's when I learned a true friend sees your art, even if you have to cross a river.

When I had stripped off my costume and put on my street clothes, I was greeted by a crush of thirsty beatniks. I was congratulated by someone who never saw the show. I was high-fived by an actor I did not know with mermaid-green hair. The word had gotten out. There was alcohol and music and assorted salty snacks at The Brick.

The plumber showed up, and I called him the plumber because he looked like a plumber, bald and bearded, and he wrote poetry that pounded hearts like a meat tenderizer. A few refugees from the Lower East Side arrived, having recently been evicted from their theatrical homes. One of them was an intense Mack truck of a man with a beard and a fondness for fedoras and Orson Welles. He was accompanied by his partner, a quiet sardonic plotter who thrived in the shadows and helped create the ambutious multimedia spectacles he wrote and directed and sometimes starred in. Eventually, I learned that he was the artist who slept inside a rat-proof chicken-wire cage in the basement of that Lower East Side theater. Alexis appeared with a slice of pizza, her trademark prop. She didn't smoke, and she didn't drink, but she loved carbohydrates. Carbohydrates and platform shoes and far-left politics.

David was buzzed and jolly, and if Michael was angry that he'd sent an inexperienced critic to review his play, no one knew it. David was a member of the Legion of Doom after all, and we were all still friends. Someone's new iPod was plugged into The Brick's sound system, and the music started, new stuff like the Yeah Yeah Yeahs and LCD Soundsystem and then The Smiths, which made me feel nauseous for a moment, until Mikki strolled over, smirking, and asked me how I was doing. I smirked back, and we stood close enough to kiss, but we knew better. I could feel her wanting to ask me what was next: Another walk in the snow? Another kiss? But I didn't know. I wasn't sure, at that point, whether or not I wanted to know.

The cast had started to unwind. Jeff was in especially good spirits because the child had been picked up by his parents, and the two would never have to see each other again. Alyssa spent the first hour of the party making the men in the cast wear the long, scratchy wig she was forced to wear as the horse, and when it was my turn, I made sure to loudly complain about the synthetic rug.

Hope and Danny seemed satisfied, as did Lawrence, who wasn't exhausted by all the young people. I made it a point to congratulate everyone in the cast, which was partly strategic: it saved me from having to talk to anyone because I was running out of things to say, and my new job was not a topic for polite society. Anyone who knew about *Maxim* didn't have anything to say other than it was sexist and homophobic and, if you were bold, that I was too good for them. But the person who would have said that would have been wrong. I was not too good for that rag.

The wine poured. I wasn't interested. I politely refused a cup filled to the brim with Merlot. The merrymaking resulted in an elbow knocking one of the bottles of plonk off a makeshift table and onto the stage with a crash and a trio of partygoers immediately dropped to their knees, giggling, and mopped up a pool of dark red vino with paper towels.

The conversation flowed. It was silly and serious, but no one talked about the lack of audience or the petty reviews. The old conundrum "if a tree falls in the forest, does it make a sound?" is a famous stumper, like "which comes first, the chicken or the egg?" There is no answer. But the question "does a play happen if no one sees it?" has a response: "yes." It does happen, even if you act in an empty theater. All voices rise to heaven.

Ivanna skillfully cornered me, which was always pleasant. She and I talked a little bit, and she delicately inquired about my relationship with Mikki. I tried to say something witty, like "a gentleman never kisses and tells," but I think I just stammered, which took her by surprise. Ivanna wasn't prying. She was too composed and thoughtful for that, and was trying to be playful. It caught me off guard, though. It shouldn't have, but it did.

Mikki saw me try to disappear into the cold, gritty bricks that made up the four walls of the theater, like a chameleon who doesn't know he hasn't blended with his surroundings. She walked over to me and gave me a hug, a deeply affectionate one. She wanted to know how I was doing, and I responded like a glum dopey teenage boy: "I'm fine, I guess. Nice party." What she wanted to know was how we were doing, if we were, in fact, that specific pronoun. Were we a thing? Were we falling in love? Were we two people together, who were kissing, constantly, exclusively, and leaving long, silly, romantic voicemails for each other, and making plans? Plans about that day, the next week, and the rest of our lives? Or were we just having a fling?

Were we a thing? It was a simple question that I couldn't answer. I deflected. I don't know what I said verbatim, but it was basically, "I don't want to talk here. I'm going to go buy some vodka at the liquor store. When I return, let's have a few more drinks and then leave." That was the important part at the end: Leave. Together. I didn't want to be presumptuous. I didn't want her to think I was angling to come over to her place. We could have walked and talked and processed our date and the chemistry and the future. I'm coming back, and then we can leave. I'm coming back for you.

This satisfied her, but I glimpsed a part of her that didn't trust me and a part that did. Mikki glowed with intelligence, and she could be cunning if she had to be, but I could feel the attraction between us, a pull, and I hadn't felt that since the first few weeks of my relationship with Julie, only what Mikki and I had, what was possible at least, would have had a chance to become something. To grow.

The party had expanded while I was making small promises to Mikki.

A director everyone knew appeared, and I think it was Hope—because Hope was the sort of person who knew things—who briefed me on her importance and how everyone knew her and respected her radical productions. Hope suggested I introduce myself, and I agreed but I didn't introduce myself because why would I do that? What would be the point? What did she have to give me? An unpaid role in a play no one would see?

She was followed shortly by a grandfatherly old jester who had spent most of the last two decades of the twentieth century high on junk but who had sobered up and transformed himself into a comedian who didn't tell jokes. A parade of subterraneans pushed through the door, one after the other: an anti-war street artist, an off-the-clock drag queen, and a peculiar young man dressed like a gentleman occultist. I safely assumed at least one of them came from money. The dancing was slowly starting, and theatre kids all dance the same way, like intoxicated temple priestesses.

The plan was to rip apart The Box the next day during strike, which is the word theatre kids use to describe the dismantling of a set. But that night, The Box was the party inside the party. Darren expressed sarcastic relief that The Box had never caught fire or collapsed and either maimed or killed everyone inside. It's not like there are any regulations for building bespoke interactive sets. The Box was a death trap, but it was our death trap.

As the bacchanalia crescendoed, I overheard plans to eat at Kellogg's Diner down the street. The word "pancakes" was being chanted, but I didn't want pancakes. I didn't want wine or light beer. And then the iPod shuffled and "One Day More" from *Les Miz* started playing, and everyone in the theater stopped what they were doing and started singing along, loudly, passionately, every emotional part, every spirited, poignant lyric about what the future holds, everyone all at once, which was my cue to walk outside and smoke.

Michael followed me. It was cold, but he was upbeat, and he thanked me. He thanked me for auditioning and being in his play, and I said, "You're welcome." That's it. I didn't thank him. I studied his nice face, and for a moment, I hated him. I hated his nice, stupid fucking face.

We stood quietly as steam leaked out of our mouths and cars whooshed by. I could hear singing and Hope's cackle through The Brick's heavy front door, the sounds of family and friendship. "Go inside," I said, "it's warm. Go inside, I'm going to run to the liquor store. I'll be right back." He opened the door, and for a brief moment, there was light and laughter, then it slammed closed behind him.

I made it half a block down the street before hailing a livery cab and telling the driver to take me to Astoria—Ditmars and 31st Street, right underneath the subway station. I watched the glittering skyscrapers of Manhattan zip past from the backseat of the Cadillac as we sailed down the BQE. He knew exactly where to deposit me.

I was greeted by name and nicknames: "Hey, boss," and "Good to see you, bro." My back was slapped. "What's new?" "Nothing." I sat at the bar and ordered a drink and another, and I don't remember when I stopped.

EPILOGUE

I spent so much of 2020 staring at delivery people through the peephole of my apartment door and at the empty subway train rumbling back and forth on its elevated track outside my third-floor window and at screens. TVs, tablets, phones. I stared at screens, and they stared back.

For months, I existed almost exclusively online, in a collective dreamscape where tens of millions of restless souls could pretend to be anyone they wanted and safely hide from a highly infectious respiratory virus that was killing thousands every week. What had once been a playground for a small but noisy community of know-it-alls in 2004 had mutated into its own massive digital reality. The internet connected families and friends across streets and oceans, but life through the looking-glass was lonely, too, and it turns out that scrolling through rage and fear for hours can make people cruel.

And it was on social media where I first learned that William Shakespeare wrote his tragedy *King Lear* while quarantined in Elizabethan London. Supposedly, the Bard banged out other timeless classics like *Macbeth* and *Antony and Cleopatra* as the deadly bubonic plague spread throughout Europe. This bit of viral historical lore was meant to be encouraging: if the greatest playwright of all time could create art during a pandemic, so could you! It was not encouraging.

I did not write a great play during the worst of the pandemic. I did not write a play. I thought about writing a play. Instead of writing, I wondered if I had any talent at all. Or if I ever did. Then, I read a quote from my old friend William Faulkner. He gave a talk at the Unversity of Virginia in 1957 and said, quite plainly, that talent doesn't matter either way. "The most important thing is insight," he said, "Curiosity to wonder, to mull, and to muse why is it that man does what he does." Well, I was doing that all the time. But still, I did not write.

I mostly swiped on my phone and grieved for everything I thought I had lost. What if I never saw a play again? I regretted growing up to become the sort of adult who pooh-poohs invitations to see a Broadway or Off-Broadway show. I had become particularly fond of calling a night at the theatre "a nap, only boring." Now I regretted ever complaining about having to sit through a play because I suddenly craved that kind of connection. I wanted to push through a lobby full of people bumping into each other like lazy pinballs to find my seat moments before curtain.

I missed the theatre. This surprised me, deeply. I longed for it, the warm, awkward closeness of it all, the sitting next to someone you do not know and briefly touching elbows on the armrest, the whispering "excuse me" when getting up, the sound of clammy hands clapping, and the inhaling and exhaling of bad breath and perfumed molecules.

I wanted to sit through a glitzy Broadway musical, romantic and silly, two hours of big grins and big voices, and I wanted to watch a serious play, a kitchen-sink tragedy, that sort of thing. There was a time I would have complained about having to endure some mid-century drama with a capital "D" but I would have gladly traded binging another mediocre streaming soap opera for a night watching actors slathered in makeup shout at each other right in front of me. God, I'd never thought I'd miss seeing spittle.

Most of all, I yearned for the poky, poorly ventilated theaters and ram-shackle performance spaces of Off-Off-Broadway and the indulgent, barely rehearsed, defiantly amateur wannabe masterpieces that played out on those stages. I never thought my heart would ache for unvarnished art, a multi-media exploration of something deeply personal or sharply political, or an inarticulate splatter of emotions expressed through subvocals and movement.

I thought about all the old theaters destroyed by progress or the pandemic. I thought about The Brick. It had survived, but barely.

Theatre wasn't the only thing I missed. I missed my local pizza shop, which had closed. They made great rice balls. I worried that my favorite bookstore wouldn't survive. I hadn't seen my mom since the lockdowns but we made it a point to try to video-call each other, which proved technologically challenging every single time; our conversations consisted mainly of me mouthing the words, "You're on mute." I missed seeing my therapist, Gary, in person.

I was unemployed and single and newly vaccinated the summer of 2021, and I spent my free time walking around the city, and I was rich with free time. I adore New York City and accept, with an open heart, that the feeling is not mutual and never will be.

I was relatively healthy, and the only substance in my bloodstream was a brand-new SSRI that was helping to calm a deep-sea treasure chest full of anxieties the pandemic had unlocked. These were hopeful but still nervous months, even though I was still wearing my mask inside grocery stores and pharmacies, and I had to show my vaccination card if I wanted to go to a movie.

So I walked. I bought a pair of fancy new sneakers from a discount website and walked. I didn't wear my mask, even though plenty of people had them on, their eyes darting back and forth, full of terror and judgment. I wore the masks indoors, but during my hikes, I pretended I was normal, that everything was the way it had been, that none of it had happened, the screaming ambulances, the bloody nose swabs, the shaky voices over the phone, calling with unbearable news.

I found myself walking by bars, which were starting to fill with people pulling their masks down to their chins and drinking. I strolled through parks and down Broadway and navigated the streets of the East Village like Pac-Man munching his way through a maze. One day, midweek, while listening to the *Les Misérables* soundtrack through my new wireless ear pods, I walked across the ugly Williamsburg Bridge from Manhattan into Brooklyn and continued to stroll.

The city was struggling to come back to life, and the streets were full of shacks hastily built by restaurants for customers who wanted the comfort of fresh air. The neighborhood had naturally changed because New York molts like a giant cosmic snake. But I still recognized Williamsburg; it was familiar to me. The neighborhood buzzed with repressed creativity and sexual fury. The bohemians were tired of drinking and partying and performing plays in the living rooms of apartments. The virus was tedious. They were impatient and starting to venture out at night and I was not invited to their parties and/ or orgies.

I walked down Union Avenue and sneered at the huge brutalist building looming over my favorite diner. Condos? Boutique hotel? I took a left on Metropolitan and considered taking the train home, but kept marching until I passed The Brick, which looked the same, except it was covered in fresh graffiti. The city had became wilder and more fragile during the plague.

During the final tumultuous months of 2020, Michael and Robert decided to step back from their artistic director roles and responsibilities and handed The Brick over to a new generation of Off-Off-Broadway theatre-makers. The deal was they'd lurk in the background and sit on the board; otherwise, an all-new staff of young, passionate artists would handle the space's day-to-day operations and creative direction.

I heard through friends that the new artistic director, Theresa, was talented, generous, a talker, a builder, and a die-hard Foreman believer who knew every silly, poetic, electrically charged art star under forty in Brooklyn. The Brick had lurched from year to year for almost two decades, barely surviving, and Theresa would continue that foolhardy tradition.

Robert was happy to return to lawyering during the day and acting, here and there, at night, the pressures of operating a small theater in constant financial peril having been relieved a bit. Michael had emailed me earlier in the year. He had created a new performance space in the basement of an apartment he was renting in Bed-Stuy, a small theater where he could continue playing. He told me to swing by whenever, and I emailed him back, telling him I would. I was trying to be more open-hearted.

The pandemic was a catastrophe but the world limped on. The digital doomsayers had predicted the theatre's demise, which did not come true. Thankfully. As it turns out, there are still people—not many—who believe, naively, despite evidence to the contrary, that theatre can change the world for the better.

I often think about all the times I declared theatre dead over mango lassis, and how I was wrong each time. The theatre will always exist so long as one person is willing to dance in the ruins.

And as I stood and stared at The Brick, a pair of theatre kids pushed the heavy door open and walked out into the dusk. They removed their masks and laughed. They both looked young, or at least younger than me. One wore a small nose ring and the other round vintage glasses. The one with glasses lit a cigarette, and I sighed. Were they actors? Was one the director? Was there a rehearsal happening inside? Was there a performance later? They started to lean into each other as the conversation turned intense and intimate, two friends whispering and hugging. The smoker took one last drag before flicking the butt toward the street while the other pulled the door back open, bowed, and gestured gracefully, as if to say: "You first."

ACKNOWLEDGMENTS

I thought the acknowledgments would be the easiest part of writing this book. I was wrong.

At first, I wrote a draft expressing heartfelt gratitude to nearly everyone I'd ever met, but that threatened to be its own book entirely. My second draft was shorter: I imagined myself winning a Tony Award and having to give a weepy thank-you speech on television in under thirty seconds.

Eventually, I found a third way: This book was written thanks to the patience and guidance of my editor, Chris Chappell, at Applause Books. To my agent and friend, David Patterson, at Stuart Krichevsky Literary Agency, thank you for years of reading insane book proposals and supporting my writing career.

To my early readers, including Robert Honeywell, Mikki Baloy, Julie Pietrangelo, Iracel Rivero, and Alexis Sottile, thanks for the kind words, encouragement, and gentle questions. A big shout-out to storytelling hotshot Maggie Cino and author Sarah Knight, whose thorough feedback was more dear and important to me than she probably knows, but she should know now.

This book was only possible thanks to long, thoughtful conversations with old friends and comrades-in-arms like Hope Cartelli, Jeff Lewonczyk, Theresa Buchheister, Michael Yawney, Alyssa Simon, Ivanna Cullinan, Moira Stone, Andy Levy, and Carla Echevarria.

The cover illustration is by my friend and longtime collaborator Carolyn Raship, who understands the triumphs and sorrows of Off-Off-Broadway.

Michael Gardner, you are a mensch. A wonderful artist but also a mensch. David Cote, let's go to another play soon. And to Bani, the Legion of Doom carries you in our collective heart.

A sincere and deeply felt thank-you to every weird little theatre kid who has ever and will ever share their art at The Brick.

As with many books, someone in the author's life has witnessed the messy, chaotic, emotionally combustible process that is writing 70,000 or so words about your life. Thank you, Ryan Selzer; you are the love of my life. Also, thank you, Morley Safer, my ten-year-old, one-eyed Shih-Tzu mutt, for licking my nose during the bleakest literary moments.

Thank you, Aida DeVore, for all the support and applause. Te amo con todo mi corazón. Thank you, Chris, for being there when I needed you. We all miss you, Dad—you and Wendy.